A Step-by-Step Guide to Reclaiming Your Power

BREAKING FREE from Narcissistic Abuse

Jaime Zuckerman, PsyD

BREAKING FREE FROM NARCISSISTIC ABUSE

Published by
Bridge City Books, an imprint of PESI Publishing, Inc.
3839 White Ave
Eau Claire, WI 54703

Cover design by Abby Isackson
Interior design by Emily Dyer
Editing by Chelsea Thompson

ISBN 9781683739548 (print)
ISBN 9781683739555 (ePUB)
ISBN 9781683739562 (ePDF)

Printed in the United States of America.

Bridge City Books

To everyone who sees themself as a survivor—

I see you, I hear you, I believe you.

Table of Contents

Introduction 1

Chapter 1. The Narcissism Surge 11

Chapter 2. The Cycle of Narcissistic Abuse 47

Chapter 3. Seeing Patterns 75

Chapter 4. Boundaries 113

Chapter 5. Narcissistic Abuse Outside of Intimate Relationships 167

Chapter 6. An ACT Approach to Narcissistic Abuse 193

Chapter 7. Escape 239

Chapter 8. Starting a New Chapter 259

Resources 275

Acknowledgments 277

About the Author 279

Introduction

It often starts with a client coming to therapy overwhelmed by the anxiety, confusion, and depression that inevitably develop within the context of a narcissistic abusive relationship. However, not every client comes to me with the understanding that they are entangled in a narcissistic abusive relationship. While some may suspect it, many can't quite articulate what is happening to them, only that they feel anxious, depressed, "crazy," ashamed, and deeply alone.

They sit across from me—some in tears, others appearing completely numb—confessing things like:

- "I don't even know who I am anymore."
- "I am a shell of who I once was."
- "I feel like I am going crazy."

What they are describing, without realizing it, are the psychological consequences of narcissistic abuse.

Unlike physical abuse, narcissistic abuse doesn't always involve what many consider to be obvious visible signs of abuse. Sometimes clients may even have trouble immediately pointing to any specific incidents within their relationship history, such as big blowout arguments. This is because the hallmark of narcissistic abuse is the slow, long-lasting, insidious erosion of a person's identity, self-worth, confidence, and ability to trust their own voice and reality.

In my almost 20 years of practicing as a licensed clinical psychologist, I have always taken a special interest in the behavior patterns of narcissistic abuse, particularly within intimate relationships and parent-child dynamics. But what truly transformed this interest into a passion was witnessing, again and again, the immense damage this type of abuse causes across generations, and how little support existed for people experiencing it.

Narcissistic abuse is often misunderstood—and it is often not talked about at all—due in large part to a superficial understanding of what characterizes a narcissist. A narcissist is often seen as someone who is selfish, loud, and perhaps in love with themself—in other words, someone immediately identifiable. While this is true for some presentations of narcissistic personality disorder, the conceptualization paints an overly simplified picture and rarely describes the more pervasive, covert forms of narcissism that I have seen in my clients' relationships over the last two decades: the gaslighting, calculated manipulation, and coercive control; the subtle yet deliberate dismantling of another's self-worth; the manufactured charm to the outside world while being abusive behind closed doors.

These clients came to me feeling confused, ashamed, and emotionally exhausted, simply trying to stay afloat within their relationship. They rarely had the language to describe what they were experiencing, but after years of manipulation and gaslighting, they'd come to believe that *they* were the problem, that if they could just try harder, communicate better, or be more supportive, things would change. But things never changed. Instead, their efforts only pushed them deeper into a very predictable, damaging cycle of narcissistic abuse and coercive control—an insidious and often invisible strategic pattern of behaviors intended to create dependency and gain control and dominance over a person while gradually stripping away their core self and autonomy.

In working with these clients, I came to realize how widespread this issue was, and how few resources existed to help them (let alone the general public) understand what was happening. I felt a deep responsibility to teach these clients that the abuse, confusion, and chaos they were facing weren't the result of their own actions, but manufactured and intentional efforts to gain control and power over their lives. I saw how critical it was to provide the knowledge and resources to these individuals, putting a name to the abuse they were enduring and validating their experiences. I wanted survivors to be heard, seen, believed, and most importantly, to feel hope.

Who Can Benefit from This Workbook

If you're reading this, chances are you suspect you may be in some form of a relationship with a narcissist. Perhaps you are certain of it, but you're unsure of where to go from here. You are trying to decipher how someone you loved, trusted, and depended on could make you feel so lost, scared, and ashamed. You've spent months, even years, trying to "fix" the relationship and "help" the other person, taking full responsibility for the problems and the conflicts and blaming yourself for being too sensitive, too crazy, or too needy.

You could have a narcissistic parent—something you've come to realize as an adult—and you are having difficulty navigating the relationship. You are still carrying around deep feelings of shame and guilt after limiting communication with your parent or cutting them off completely, and you can't seem to be able to resolve these painful feelings.

Or maybe you have a loved one who you believe to be in a narcissistic abusive relationship, but you don't know how to help them. You feel scared, frustrated, and maybe even helpless. Your efforts to communicate your concerns, argue your points, or convince your loved one to leave have all been unsuccessful. In fact, they've seemed to make the situation worse, drawing an even bigger wedge between you and them.

Whether you're an intimate partner, a spouse, a colleague, a family member, or a friend, you're not wrong for feeling the way you are feeling: It is exactly what a narcissistic abuser wants you to feel.

No matter the role a narcissist plays in your life, the impact of the relationship can be profound and long-lasting, affecting your mental, physical, and emotional health. Approaching these complex dynamics with targeted strategies geared specifically to the nuances and complexities of narcissistic abuse is essential to preserving self-identity and reducing the risks of isolation, self-doubt, fear, physical illness, and confusion that so often follow.

A relationship like this isn't just "challenging" or "toxic." It is not the result of poor communication, a lack of compromise, different love languages, or stubborn family members. Moreover, the problems aren't going to get better, even if you try to be more understanding of where they're coming from, communicate your feelings better, or work on your own unhealthy patterns or negative beliefs about yourself. The issue in your relationship is a *power and control imbalance* in which one person is deliberately attempting to manipulate, isolate, and assert dominance over you. Their goal isn't to find ways to improve communication or compromise—it is to slowly break your spirit.

After conversations with hundreds of clients over the years, I felt compelled to bring this information to the masses. The time has come to go beyond one-on-one support for my clients and offer a form of "preventive medicine" for this complex presentation of abuse—a way to help people identify the early warning signs of coercive control and narcissistic abuse in their relationships.

Using a behavioral approach consisting of mindfulness, cognitive defusion techniques, and the importance of values-driven actions, I help survivors learn to observe their thoughts and feelings without becoming consumed by them. I guide them in recognizing the patterns of narcissistic abuse so they can better understand what drives the narcissist's behaviors, anticipate future behaviors, and set effective boundaries in response to the behaviors. This work not only empowers these clients to navigate an abusive relationship, but also helps them regain their sense of self, learn to live in the present moment rather than in survival mode, and live a fulfilled and values-driven life.

Acceptance and Commitment Therapy: A Different Approach

Many of you reading this have already sought some form of help through individual therapy, couples therapy, or family therapy, hoping things would finally make sense or begin to change for the better. You've read countless books, listened to numerous podcasts, and followed dozens of experts online. You've confided in trusted family and friends. After all of this, you've ended up feeling even more confused and invalidated.

If you find this relatable, it is only natural to ask yourself how this book could offer you something different, especially if what you've tried thus far hasn't truly stuck. The difference begins with understanding that the dynamics of narcissistic abuse struggle to fit within the same therapeutic lens as other forms of toxic relationships.

Many existing therapy approaches focus on *dual accountability* in relationships—that is, the way both partners contribute to the relationship's problems—and use techniques such as joint communication improvement, healthy conflict resolution, and an understanding of how one's patterns impact the relationship. While these techniques are effective in treating other types of diagnoses and relationship difficulties, they should not, and cannot, be the focus of therapy for narcissistic abuse survivors. They don't need in-depth explorations on how to "fix" the relationship. What they *do* need are concrete strategies tailored specifically to the narcissist's manipulation and control in order to identify and predict patterns of coercive control, establish boundaries and effective responses, and formulate a tangible action plan that works long term. It is only after these skills have been developed, independent of the narcissist, that a survivor can begin to recreate an accurate self-narrative and eventually reclaim their power, identity, and autonomy.

Many traditional therapeutic frameworks do not sufficiently recognize the fundamental ways narcissistic abuse and coercive control differ from other relationship difficulties, nor do they incorporate these differences as part of the foundation of their treatment approaches, something that is essential to helping survivors develop the skills necessary to move forward and rediscover their sense of self.

This is where acceptance and commitment therapy (ACT) becomes a critical component in the process of healing from narcissistic abuse. ACT places heavy emphasis on the importance of values—and aligning behaviors with those values. After first identifying your values (e.g., "I value being present as a parent"), you can use these values as anchor points as you navigate this complex relationship.

ACT and mindfulness-based approaches also reduce your emotional, cognitive, and behavioral reactivity to the confusion and chaos that a narcissistic abuser strives to create. The more you learn to mentally untangle yourself from their actions, words, and manipulation, the better you can resist their attempts to stir up your emotions and undermine your confidence. As you practice these strategies, your trust in your perception of reality will strengthen, opening your eyes to the patterns of the narcissist's behavior. Over time, this will allow you to predict their tactics and respond with intention rather than emotion.

Finally, ACT helps you recognize that the narcissist's manipulative efforts are not a reflection of your worth—that, despite what they may have told you to believe about yourself, you possess your own self-narrative separate from the narcissist. You are inherently worthy, capable, and deserving of the life you want for yourself. This realization, combined with aligning your actions with what you value most, is what empowers you to take the necessary steps toward healing, even in the face of fear, shame, confusion, and sadness.

While pain, fear, and shame may remain with survivors of narcissistic abuse, it doesn't have to drive their behaviors and choices or define their future. I have seen clients in decades-long narcissistic abusive relationships, who gave up their careers, isolated themselves from family and friends, and completely lost their sense of self, go on to rediscover their purpose, build meaningful connections, and live successful and healthy lives. One former client eventually went back to finish her graduate degree and launched a successful law practice. I've seen numerous adult children of narcissistic parents consciously break the cycle of abuse and go on to nurture healthy, loving relationships with their own kids. And I have witnessed clients who, after escaping their abusers, eventually reentered the dating world and found healthy relationships. The ACT- and mindfulness-based practices that helped a person break free from the narcissist's influence ultimately become the foundation for a fulfilling, authentic life.

ACT Concept

ACT for Narcissistic Abuse

ACT is an incredibly effective tool for helping survivors of narcissistic abuse. As the strategies in this book center on the ACT principles, specific ACT concepts have been highlighted throughout. Chapter 6 contains exercises that develop and expand on these concepts, which can help you gradually reclaim your power, gain confidence, and move closer to a fulfilled life reflective of your true self.

This book is a practical resource for anyone impacted by narcissistic abuse, offering validation of your experience and actionable steps for navigating and healing from these complex and traumatic relationships. It will also serve those who wish to better understand narcissistic abuse, whether for the purpose of protecting yourself or supporting a survivor. Drawing on evidence-based techniques, such as value identification, grounding exercises, breathwork, cognitive defusion, mindfulness, and more, this workbook guides you to identify patterns, establish healthy boundaries, act in alignment with your values, and take steps toward healing from the harm caused by your relationship. Through real-life scenarios, pattern- and behavior-tracking tools, and guided reflection prompts, you will learn how to safely navigate narcissistic relationships, break free from coercively controlling behaviors, and begin the healing process.

My hope for this book is to provide the language for the painful experiences and emotions you've endured, help you recognize the narcissist's manipulative tactics and patterns of control, and reveal the blueprint of their abuse. Most importantly, these pages will equip you with the skills to set and maintain effective boundaries so that, over time, you can restore your sense of self, feel empowered in your truth, and truly believe that none of this was your fault.

You're not crazy.

You're not too sensitive.

You're not alone.

You can move forward.

1

The Narcissism Surge

Why does it seem as if there are suddenly so many narcissists walking among us?

In recent years, social media has provided a powerful outlet for people to share their experiences with narcissistic abuse, tell their stories of survival, and speak their truth. Bringing these experiences to light has empowered many who suffer in silence to reclaim their sense of worth and dignity, and most importantly, realize that they are not alone. But this surge in awareness is not just validating for survivors; it is quite literally saving lives.

At the same time, social media content tends to oversimplify the definition of narcissism and narcissistic abuse. At best, a loose application of the term creates harmful misconceptions about narcissistic abuse and its seriousness. At worst, it contributes to a perception that the word *narcissist* is just a trending form of weaponized therapy-speak and a catchall phrase to describe any individual who exhibits behaviors such as arrogance, entitlement, low empathy, or self-importance. This perception may influence survivors to remain silent, fearing their experience will be dismissed and they will be judged for overreacting.

Increased awareness is only half the battle. There's still a pressing need for accurate information about narcissism, narcissistic abuse, and coercive control. This is essential not only for those who are currently experiencing narcissistic abuse and coercively controlling behaviors, but also for people in positions to recognize, validate, and help abuse survivors. This includes mental health providers, law enforcement, family courts, and health care providers. Therefore, it makes sense to begin with a thorough understanding of what does and doesn't define true narcissism.

What Narcissism Is (and Isn't)

Narcissistic personality disorder (NPD) is a complex personality disorder with a specific and multilayered behavioral presentation. The *Diagnostic and Statistical Manual of Mental Disorders, Fifth Edition, Text Revision* (*DSM-5-TR*) defines NPD as a pervasive personality style characterized by extreme interpersonal dysfunction across all aspects of a person's life, beginning in early adulthood. It is marked by intense grandiosity, a sense of entitlement, exaggerated self-importance, and a chronic need for admiration and recognition—even when such responses are not warranted. People with NPD are interpersonally exploitative, seeking power and dominance through highly controlling and manipulative behaviors without remorse or empathy for the harm they cause others.

People often wonder if their partner or family member could be a clinical narcissist. This person may be overbearing, selfish, and undeniably difficult to be around. They might repeatedly promise to change and never follow through. Their behaviors may even be reminiscent of some of the previous criteria, but this is not an automatic confirmation that they have NPD.

With the rise in narcissism exposure, it's not surprising that we are experiencing increased discussion about the disorder as a whole. But turning a clinical diagnosis into a trendy catchall description of difficult or even toxic behavior is harmful and ultimately waters down the diagnosis. It has dire implications for the individual in a relationship with someone who has NPD. It undermines the serious nature of their experiences, leading others to dismiss reports of narcissistic abuse as an overreaction, a cursory explanation, or a bid for attention. Consequently, those who are being abused feel increasingly invalidated and scared, making it far less likely they will seek the support they desperately need.

So how can we *really* tell if someone is truly a narcissist or just selfish and difficult?

All Narcissists Are Jerks, But Not All Jerks Are Narcissists

Just as clinical narcissism doesn't always present as obviously overbearing and selfish behavior, overbearing and selfish behavior doesn't always indicate that someone is a narcissist. As skeptics rightly point out, someone breaking up with you without a "good" reason doesn't make them a narcissist; your coworker's constant bragging doesn't make them a narcissist; a parent's tendency to criticize or make passive-aggressive comments doesn't make them a narcissist. These behaviors are off-putting and hurtful, but in isolation, they are not always indicative of narcissistic abuse.

All of us are prone, in certain situations or stages of life, to act selfishly or overstate our accomplishments. These behaviors can be the result of immaturity, anxiety, ambition, or learned patterns of problem-solving. At their core, however, they are not guided by a conscious effort to control another person. NPD, on the other hand, is a deep-rooted, pervasive personality style marked by a lack of empathy, a need for constant control and power over another person, manipulation, entitlement, and a refusal to take personal accountability for their harmful behaviors. It's not something they can "grow out of" or change by seminal life lessons or heart-to-heart talks.

You Can't Be a Narcissist Some of the Time

Someone with a true diagnosis of NPD does not possess one singular maladaptive character trait, like being self-absorbed with their own accomplishments or shutting down and going silent during arguments. Rather, as shown in the *DSM* definition, narcissists present with a cluster of specific personality traits and relational behaviors. Furthermore, a narcissist's behaviors do not present only in specific contexts with specific people; they are static, chronic, and pervasive within all domains of life. While a narcissist may present outwardly as charming, caring, and genuinely helpful, it is a facade used to mask their deliberate efforts to gain total control and dominance over another person while gradually limiting their independence and self-identity. Their manipulation and abusive behaviors reflect a long-standing and pervasive dysfunctional pattern of interpersonal behaviors woven throughout *all* their relationships *all* of the time.

A Narcissist's Behavior Isn't Accidental or Aimless

We all demonstrate toxic behaviors at times—we are human. We may even have a history of unhealthy behavior patterns from childhood that we carried into adulthood. For example, say as a child you were taught that expressing emotions is a form of weakness. Any expression of sadness or fear was met with verbal attacks: "Just get over it" or "Real men don't cry." To avoid this punishment, you learned to keep your emotions hidden and sought to be rewarded for being "strong." It worked for you then, but as an adult, this pattern of behavior has negatively influenced your relationships, as you frequently shut people out and push them away. It wasn't until recently, however, that you were made aware of how often these patterns arise and how they negatively impact those you care about. This causes you tremendous guilt and shame, as the last thing you ever wanted to do was hurt others. You take accountability for the pain you've caused, and you seek therapy to change your toxic patterns, as you do not want to hurt anyone else in your life.

Someone with NPD may display behaviors that, on the surface, resemble the unhealthy pattern previously described. However, what makes a narcissist's behaviors inherently different is their underlying purpose and motive. A narcissist's behavior patterns are strategic attempts to control, manipulate, and gain power over you; they are not unknowingly repeating learned patterns. Their actions are aimed at creating dependency by slowly eroding your identity, autonomy, and agency. Unlike the previous scenario, someone with NPD does not feel guilt, empathy, or remorse for any pain they cause, does not take accountability even when confronted, and has no intention of changing their behavior. In other words, they are not bothered by the interpersonal dysfunction and harm their actions have caused. In fact, they use the emotions of others as a tool of manipulation.

Whether they present themself as generous and loving, play the mistreated victim, lash out with rageful outbursts, or subtly undermine you with passive-aggressive digs and the silent treatment, a narcissist's behaviors are manipulative tools for getting what we call *narcissistic supply*. "Supply" refers to anything that fuels the narcissist's ego; gains them access to your emotions, thoughts, and actions; and satisfies their need for control, power, and dominance. Supply can be gained by eliciting admiration, attention, or validation, but it could just as easily be acquired by provoking painful emotions, stirring up drama, or nudging a complicated situation into chaos. A narcissist may get supply in one moment by acting like a caring, doting spouse in front of friends and neighbors, while in the next moment they send an upsetting text just as you're about to give an important presentation at work.

This concept can be difficult to comprehend; after all, most people's behaviors align with their intentions. If your partner tells you they didn't love the dinner you made, it's because they didn't like the dinner. If your parent says they want you to come home for Thanksgiving, it's because they miss you and want to spend time with you. But for someone with NPD, the purpose of their behavior is much more insidious. It's not about the dinner you cooked or where you go for the holidays; it's about gaining control and power over what you do, how you think, and, more importantly, how you feel about yourself.

Imagine that a mother scolds her teenage son because he forgot to take the trash out. In most cases, this commonplace conflict is the result of the mother's real frustration about the trash, or about her growing child's unwillingness to take responsibility for a chore. For a narcissistic mother, however, the issue isn't the trash. Perhaps earlier that day, the teen received an acceptance letter to a college across the country. The child's success, along with his excitement about it, is perceived by the narcissistic mother as direct abandonment and disrespect. Rather than showing vulnerability by admitting her fear of being lonely, she tries to regain her perceived loss of control by taking the focus away from her child's important moment and undermining his confidence about moving toward an autonomous adulthood: "You think you're ready to move out on your own? You can't even remember to take the trash out! I put up with this because I'm your mother, but a college roommate would kick you out." When a narcissist perceives a loss of control, they will engage in whatever behaviors help them regain their power. This can range from excessive apologies and gift giving to silent treatments or physical abuse. While the behaviors appear different on the surface, the underlying purpose is the same—to manipulate and regain control.

What Is Narcissistic Abuse?

When clients enter therapy with me, many of them are completely unaware of the true complexity of the abuse they are experiencing. They may know something feels "off," but they are unable to articulate why they feel this way. Many clients in this situation come to therapy with a strong belief that they are the problem in the relationship, seeking help for what they believe to be anxiety, depression, and confusion. Some clients even report feeling as if they are "going crazy." It never occurs to them that the source of their psychological, cognitive, and emotional difficulties (not to mention their sleep problems and physical health concerns) could be a long-standing pattern of abusive behavior by the very person with whom they are in a relationship. In order to truly comprehend what narcissistic abuse is, it is essential to first understand the concept of *coercive control.*

Coercive Control

Coercive control is the underlying basis for all forms of narcissistic abusive behavior. It is subtle and gradual, leaving many survivors unaware that what they are experiencing *is* abuse. It may come in the form of passive-aggressive digs, love bombing after an argument, protective concern, and being given the silent treatment—all happening in just a day or two. It may look like someone scolding you for not being more confident in yourself, only to cut you down publicly when you receive a compliment. Coercive control quietly chips away at your sense of self so that you increasingly rely on the abuser to dictate your actions, validate your thoughts and feelings, and manufacture your self-identity.

We typically understand abuse as external attacks, such as physical violence, sexual assault, or blatant verbal insults, which may or may not follow a specific pattern. Coercive control, on the other hand, is a gradually occurring, often invisible, strategic pattern of systemic abuse and manipulation designed to gain power, control, and dominance over another person. This kind of control infiltrates your daily life, slowly eroding your agency, autonomy, and sense of self over time. Every aspect of your life is tightly controlled and heavily scrutinized.

These behaviors often occur in subtle, pervasive patterns and manifest as various forms of abuse that can be difficult to recognize. While perceived to occur most often within intimate relationships, coercive control is at the core of all forms of narcissistic abuse, including psychological abuse, emotional abuse, sexual abuse, financial abuse, legal abuse, and others.

How Narcissistic Abuse Shows Up

Narcissistic abuse is a form of interpersonal abuse that can manifest in various ways. The primary aim of a narcissistic abuser is to gain power, control, and dominance over you while stripping away your self-identity through a variety of abusive and manipulative strategies.

The narcissist's use of manipulative tactics follows a very specific playbook, beginning at the onset of a relationship and unfolding in a highly predictable progression across its lifespan, often persisting even after the relationship ends. At the start of a relationship, the narcissist methodically uses tactics to cultivate trust, identify your vulnerabilities, and slowly craft doubt in your perception of reality. As time goes on, the abuser chips away at these elements, seeking to increase access to all emotional, cognitive, and psychological function so that they can control each facet of your life.

Narcissistic abuse often goes unnoticed for long periods of time, not just by the person experiencing it firsthand but also by those around them. The constant fear, confusion, isolation, and dependency, coupled with occasional sprinklings of what looks like love, concern, and kindness, keeps you emotionally invested, hanging on to the hope of change even as you feel your own identity and autonomy draining away. This seemingly unpredictable pattern of abuse also makes it nearly impossible to explain what's happening to anyone outside the immediate relationship. Even long after the relationship ends, many survivors still struggle to understand the relationship and label it as abusive.

This is why learning to recognize these tactics and behavioral patterns is crucial not only for identifying and navigating narcissistic abuse, but also for avoiding these relationships entirely.

Psychological Abuse

The most common hallmark of narcissistic abuse is psychological abuse, a form marked by a deliberate effort to gain control by instilling profound fear, confusion, and self-doubt in you. Common psychological abuse strategies include social isolation, intimidation, and gaslighting—that is, the abuser will, over time, convince you that your friends and family do not have your best interest at heart, are jealous of the relationship, and can't be trusted. The narcissist will keep you in a state of dread and uncertainty by deliberately undermining your trust in your own reality.

Gaslighting

While we often hear the term *gaslighting* used interchangeably with lying, the purpose of the two are inherently different. Lying is saying something untrue to avoid consequences or get something you want. But when confronted with evidence against their lie, most liars are forced to come clean. Gaslighting, however, is a calculated form of psychological manipulation with the primary goal of distorting your perception of reality and making you doubt your own thoughts, feelings, and personal judgment. Gaslighting leaves you confused, scared, and dependent on the gaslighter to define reality for you. When challenged with facts, a gaslighter will not come clean, but instead deflect blame, twist words, and continue to alter the narrative.

For example, say that your partner agreed to attend an important work dinner with you. You both decided it made the most sense to meet there after work, but on the night of the dinner, your partner never shows up. You call and text repeatedly but are unable to reach them. Worried sick, you rush home and find them sprawled on the couch, watching TV and eating from a takeout container. Torn between fury and relief, you blurt out how hurt and anxious you've been, and demand to know why they didn't show up.

In this situation, gaslighting might sound like this: "What are you talking about? I never told you I was coming. You told me you had a dinner, but you never asked me! You always twist things around to make it my fault. How do you think I felt not being included in your big plans? Did you ever think about that? No, because all you care about is yourself and your job."

They aren't just lying; they are trying to control the narrative, making you doubt your perception, your memory of events, and the way you feel. Even when a gaslighter is faced with blatant evidence that contradicts their narrative, they will continue to insist that you're wrong, that you're crazy, that you're at fault. They may even invent more lies to "explain away" the evidence they've been shown. Before you realize it, you're apologizing profusely for not communicating your plans well and for how much you've hurt *them*.

Over time, gaslighting slowly erodes even the most confident person's ability to trust their own perception of reality and, with it, their self-identity. You become so completely dependent on your abuser's version of events because you've been manipulated into not trusting your own. Needless to say, that is a very scary place to be.

Another common tactic of psychological abuse is extreme monitoring. For example, the narcissist might force you to get permission to make plans or spend money, provide all the details of any outings outside the home, or give them your login and password information. It may even become extremely granular; you may need to check in every few minutes via text or consult the abuser about everyday personal decisions, like what to wear or eat. Psychological abusers may also demand "proof" of loyalty by subjecting you to arbitrary tests, such as feigning sickness on a night you are going out with friends to see if you choose to stay home, or asking you to perform favors that compromise your safety or dignity (e.g., sending them nude photos of yourself or recording your conversations about sensitive topics). This gives them leverage if in the future you do not abide by their rules or you attempt to end the relationship.

Over time, this form of abuse can break down your entire sense of identity. I often hear clients who have been involved in narcissistic abusive relationships say that they feel like a shell of their former self. After years of being fed a deliberately manufactured narrative that told them who and what they were expected to be, they no longer know who they are, what their interests are, and what's really important to them in life. The fear of making the wrong decision (i.e., doing something that went against the narcissist's narrative) was terrifying for them. Adhering to the narrative had become a necessary survival skill, keeping them stuck in the relationship while also making them feel as if they were slowly losing themself.

One of the reasons psychological abuse is so difficult to identify is the survivor's inability to recognize that it is even happening. This is because psychological abuse can occur in extremely subtle and insidious ways. At the onset of the relationship, the abuser presents a facade of concern, interest, helpfulness, and love, while quietly planting seeds of self-doubt and a mistrust of anyone and anything outside the relationship. Slowly but surely, you become increasingly isolated from your social network, ultimately developing a dependency on the abuser to make decisions, shape your identity, and define your reality. Needless to say, this is a significant barrier when it comes to escaping the relationship.

Emotional Abuse

Emotional abuse refers to a consistent and repetitive pattern of efforts to dismantle your confidence, self-esteem, and mental wellness by manipulating and exploiting your emotions. One common strategy is for the abuser to invoke guilt out of your love and commitment to them, making you feel selfish for having your own needs, disloyal for having a different opinion, or unsupportive for pursuing your individual goals and interests. Shame is another power tactic used by narcissistic abusers; they might repeatedly remind you of times when you've failed, or inflate the significance of a mild embarrassment.

Like with psychological abuse, shame is a particularly effective way for the abuser to isolate you from your support network. Shame is a silencer, leading you to distance yourself from others and hide what is happening in your life and what you're feeling. Naturally, the most common piece of information that stays hidden is the fact that you are suffering the abuse. This is why emotional abuse is one of the most significant deterrents to leaving a relationship or cutting ties with a narcissist.

Because of the nonphysical nature of narcissistic abuse, it is common for people to minimize their experience of abuse. It can be hard to identify even in the moment it's occurring because the abuser will often mask it within the context of blame. They might accuse you of being the "reason" for their behavior (e.g., "I hate saying things like this, but your thoughtlessness brings out the worst in me"). Meanwhile, when you try to assert your feelings in response to their behavior, they will typically resort to gaslighting ("I was just joking") or making you feel as though you have no right to your own emotions ("You're so sensitive that it's impossible to have fun with you"). This can make it even more likely that you will minimize your experience, both publicly and in your own mind. To preserve peace, avoid conflict, or simply survive your day-to-day life, you may silence your own needs, do your best to appease the abuser, and adopt the abuser's distorted narrative, leading to the gradual erosion of your sense of self.

Your Emotional Reflex

If you are questioning whether what you are experiencing is emotional abuse, a helpful first step is to check in with your initial emotional responses—what I refer to as your *emotional reflex*. Do you feel panicked? Anxious? On edge? For those who have difficulty identifying emotions, focus on how your body feels instead. Do you feel tension in certain parts of your body throughout the day, or in situations with a specific person? If so, where do you feel the tension, and what does it feel like?

If these are the immediate responses that arise for you, you may be experiencing emotional abuse. It is important to notice these immediate emotions and physical sensations. They ground you in the present moment and provide a degree of clarity that helps you validate your own emotions and begin to question the accuracy of the abuser's narrative.

Sexual Abuse

Typically, when people hear the term *sexual abuse*, they think of two scenarios: rape by a stranger or childhood sexual abuse. However, sexual abuse also exists within intimate partnerships, often manifesting in subtle, coercive ways that many fail to recognize as abuse, including the survivors themselves.

To better understand this form of abuse, known as *sexual coercion,* it is first necessary to gain insight into how narcissists view sex. For a narcissist, sex has very little to do with establishing intimate bonds, developing deep emotions, or even feeling real pleasure—it is about power and control. It is used as a tool to feed their constant need for validation and self-gratification and as a tactic to manipulate your emotions, often by instilling shame and guilt. Narcissists view their partners as sexual objects, existing solely to gratify their own needs. Because they feel entitled to sex on their terms—whenever, however, and wherever they want it—they are persistent and highly manipulative in their attempts to get you to engage in sexual activity. The coercion shows up in behaviors like repeatedly asking you to engage in sexual activity until you give in or putting you in an unwanted situation (e.g., deliberately getting into bed naked with the expectation of sex despite not having asked for it, trying a new position or act without consent). Common justifications for this behavior include statements such as "If you loved me, you would ____" or "Don't be such a prude—this is what couples do!"

These manipulative behaviors often grow more extreme over time. The abuser may purposely wake you up at 2 a.m. to pick a fight, then tell you that if you perform a certain sexual act, they will stop screaming and let you go back to bed. The abuser may withhold something you need, such as keys to the car or your cell phone, until you unwillingly "agree" to some sexual favor. Eventually, you might come to see sex as transactional rather than relational, the only way to keep peace in the relationship.

Sexual coercion can also involve withholding sex. For example, if the abuser wants something (sexual or otherwise) from you, they may threaten to go elsewhere for sex if they don't get what they want. This is often accompanied by derogatory comments about your appearance or insults regarding your sexual performance. They may also withhold sex without explanation to make you think you did something to anger them. All of this is used to break down your self-esteem.

These abusive patterns of behavior can be especially difficult to identify, particularly within marriages; this often results in tremendous confusion, shame, and guilt for survivors. Many people caught in these dynamics do not see it for what it is: a blatant violation of their boundaries. The telltale sign of sexual abuse and coercion is that it has little to do with pleasure or intimacy, and everything to do with obtaining power and control, and asserting dominance over another human being.

Financial Abuse

Financial abuse can occur across all relationship types, including intimate, family, and work. It involves deliberate and strategic control over another's financial resources and decision-making abilities. Financial abuse often makes it incredibly difficult for you to access financial resources or cuts them off completely. It is also common for a narcissistic abuser to, over time, instill doubt in your perceived ability to manage your money or make any financial decisions. This deepens your dependency on the narcissist, making it extremely difficult to leave the relationship.

In romantic relationships, financial abuse often begins early, masked as acts of generosity, helpfulness, and concern. For example, if an abuser knows you are having financial difficulties, they may offer to pay for major expenses, such as rent or car payments, or even suggest you cancel your credit cards and use theirs instead. As the relationship progresses, they may suggest giving up your home to move in with them, offer to manage your money for you, make investments on your behalf with your own finances, or even propose that you quit your job entirely so that they can support you. These strategies are typically presented as a reflection of the relationship's strong bond and potential longevity.

But what is initially presented as acts of care and thoughtfulness are simply tools to coerce you into giving up your financial independence. Initially, the abuser may justify their actions as being helpful by lifting the burden off you, but over time, they convince you that you're incapable of managing finances and are fiscally irresponsible. The abuser may put you on a restrictive "allowance," insist you show proof of all your transactions, or force you to ask for money, even for basic purchases such as a haircut or gas for your car. Meanwhile, it's common for the abuser to gamble, overspend, and take out loans, home equity lines, and credit cards in your name without your knowledge. They will arbitrarily withhold money, not only to manipulate you into doing what they want, but also to cultivate extreme anxiety and a state of helplessness and reliance that makes you easier to manipulate and control. Slowly and discreetly, they restrict your financial independence and make you increasingly dependent on them; this loss of financial freedom is one of the primary reasons so many survivors remain trapped in abusive relationships.

Financial abuse isn't relegated to intimate partnerships. Narcissistic parents often weaponize finances to manipulate and control their family members. Any step their child takes toward autonomy is viewed as a sign of disrespect, abandonment, and a threat to the narcissist's control, and finances are a tool the narcissistic parent uses to maintain that control. Along with withholding access to funds and convincing the child that they are incapable of managing their own finances, the narcissistic parent may utilize money—or promises of money—to not only hinder their child's independence but also promote rivalry between siblings.

Finances are simply another vehicle the narcissist uses to obtain power and control while simultaneously stripping you of your independence, decision-making capacity, and ultimately, your ability to leave the relationship. It creates a vicious cycle of control and dependency that can be extremely difficult—and scary—to break.

Legal Abuse

Legal abuse occurs when the narcissistic abuser uses the legal system to intimidate and control your time, money, and energy. It can take several forms, such as continuous filing of false claims and groundless restraining orders, the routine threat of lawsuits, custody battles, demanding psychological and vocational evaluations, and taking other unnecessary legal actions that require you to attend repeated court hearings, respond to legal requests, and spend a considerable amount of money. These excessive and lengthy litigation demands cause financial and emotional overwhelm, draining you of time and resources and breaking down your psychological well-being—all with the primary goal of taking power and control away from you. In doing so, their hope is that you become so psychologically and financially exhausted that you will concede to their narrative and demands.

They, too, will drain enormous amounts of money, time, and energy, yet seem unfazed by these losses, all because their need for total power and control outweighs all other consequences. Remaining relevant and in control is far more important to the narcissist, as their self-worth is deeply intertwined with maintaining their perceived position of power. The ongoing legal chaos they create is a direct source of narcissistic supply—they are addicted to it.

Therefore, narcissists love to use the legal system as their stage, particularly within the family courts. They have no trouble performing the part of a caring parent, a hurting spouse, or a fair-minded person who just wants what is owed to them. Within the context of narcissistic abuse, we see legal abuse occur most often during divorce and custody proceedings. Even in divorces with children involved, narcissists will not hesitate to use their own children as pawns in their effort to punish and control their ex-partner. Knowing you will go to any length to protect your children gives them easy leverage and access to your emotions. They may threaten to take full custody, bad-mouth you to the children, and even accuse you of neglect, abuse, and mental instability in order to create a false narrative of your unfitness as a caregiver. Because of their lack of empathy, they view your suffering as a victory, even if they are self-destructing other areas of their own life—and even at the expense of their own child.

REFLECTION

Learning to identify the various forms of narcissistic abuse allows you to see the calculated patterns of coercively controlling behavior within the relationship dynamic rather than a randomly occurring event or the result of something you did wrong. Because survivors are taught to distrust their own reality, having the language to name your experiences can help create space between yourself and the narcissist's false narrative you have been conditioned to accept as truth. Your reactions are not "crazy" or "dramatic." They are appropriate responses to abusive behaviors. Identifying patterns of abuse also gives language to something that often feels impossible to communicate to others.

The following case examples demonstrate the different forms of narcissistic abuse we've discussed so far. After reading each example, record the type of abuse present in the relationship.

David and Melissa

Melissa and her husband, David, were at an award ceremony, where a large group of educators was celebrating Melissa with the honor of Outstanding Teacher of the Year. But during the post-ceremony cocktail reception, David became highly intoxicated, causing quite a disruption for the other guests. Because of his inappropriate behavior, David was asked to leave the event. Out of a sense of obligation, Melissa decided to skip the rest of her own event and escort David home, apologizing on his behalf to the event organizers and guests as she left.

During the drive home, David became furious with Melissa, accusing her of leaving him alone at their table with "idiots" whom he had "nothing in common with." He went on to say that her self-absorption was what caused him to drink so much. What else, he demanded, was he supposed to do when he was so bored? Used to such egregious behavior by her husband, Melissa silently prayed that he would pass out as soon as they got home.

However, rather than causing him to pass out, the alcohol was fueling his outrage. David continued to scream at Melissa, now adding false accusations that she probably received the award because she slept with her boss. The screaming went on for hours until, around 2 a.m., David asserted that the only way he could calm down was if Melissa would "just have sex with him already."

By this point, Melissa had locked herself in the spare bedroom in hopes of getting some sleep. This didn't stop David from continuing to cause absolute chaos; he banged on the door, alternating between insincere apologies and calling Melissa a horrible wife who never supported him. This carried on for two more hours, until Melissa was mentally and physically exhausted. With tears in her eyes, she opened the door and walked past David, who stood there with wide eyes and arms crossed, into their shared bedroom. As they both got into bed, David turned to Melissa and, with a smile on his face, said, "Make-up sex is the best, isn't it?"

What type of abuse is most prominent in this scenario?

____

What specific patterns of behavior led you to this conclusion?

____

____

____

Sandra and Will

Sandra had been convinced for some time that her boyfriend of four years, Will, had been cheating on her. There had been so many clues over the years of their relationship, but none that she could prove with certainty. Anytime Sandra mentioned her suspicions to Will, it was met with a forceful denial that often led to an argument and, sometimes, the silent treatment for days afterward. Over the years, Sandra realized that keeping her doubts to herself was much easier than arguing with her boyfriend. One evening, however, while Will was in the shower, she noticed that he had left his phone charging in the kitchen. She decided to look for solid proof of Will's infidelity. There would be no denying against hard facts like pictures and text messages from other women.

Sandra cautiously picked up Will's phone and entered his passcode. (She had watched him one time over his shoulder while he entered it.) As she began going through his texts and pictures, her heart sank into her stomach. There it was, in plain sight: a handful of sexual correspondences between Will and several other women, some with which she was even friendly. At first glance, it appeared the messages dated back to well over a year ago. She had been right all along but was holding on to the hope that she was being crazy and paranoid, just like Will had always told her.

Sandra was so consumed with Will's phone that she didn't notice him approach until he was standing in front of her. Startled, Sandra dropped the phone, and Will swooped in to pick it up. He immediately accused her of being disrespectful of his belongings and said she was delusional to go through his personal communication. He continued to berate her, telling her she was paranoid, pathetic, and in need of psychiatric medication.

Sandra started to cry, screaming at him that she had known all along he had been cheating on her, and now finally had the proof. However, the more Sandra argued her points, the more Will simply accused her of being "crazy," telling her the texts and pictures in his phone were not even his. The pictures of women were taken off the internet, he claimed, and it was something "all guys do." He told her to stop being so dramatic and possessive. When Sandra asked specifically about the pictures that he was in with another woman, Will told her it wasn't him. He insisted that she couldn't possibly have gotten a good enough look while quickly scrolling through, that her preconceived notion that it was him, coupled with her paranoia, had tricked her brain into assuming it was him.

When confronted with the slew of sexual text messages, he confidently explained how his friend had asked him to hide those messages and pictures on his phone so his friend's wife wouldn't find them. Will then proceeded to call Sandra a "homewrecker," stating that his friend's marriage would now be ruined because of her.

For every piece of evidence Sandra presented, Will had an answer and explanation. Sandra's sense of doubt began to creep in. She was, after all, purposely searching for evidence; maybe this bias clouded her perception. Maybe Will was just being a good friend by keeping those pictures safe? Sandra certainly didn't want to break up anyone else's marriage! What if Sandra was wrong? What if Will was correct that Sandra's "obsession" with proving his infidelity clouded her judgment. Now what?

As the argument continued, the energy began to shift. It wasn't long before extreme doubt consumed Sandra, and she began to apologize to Will. She took accountability for starting an argument based on false evidence, and she admitted that her love for Will could sometimes cause her considerable worry. She apologized for going through his phone without his awareness, and subsequently, accepted Will's narrative that she was crazy and likely needed to be on psychiatric medication. Will went on to say that Sandra's accusations had really upset him, and because of this, he needed to go away on a boys' trip to Vegas to clear his head and think about their relationship. He also changed the password on his phone so Sandra could not have the opportunity to accuse him of any wrongdoings again.

What type of abuse is most prominent in this scenario?

____

What specific behaviors led you to this conclusion?

____

____

____

Dara and Francis

From the moment Dara met Francis, she felt it was love at first sight—a "cosmic connection" is how they both described it to people. It didn't take long before Francis asked Dara to move in with him. At his suggestion, she willingly sold her apartment. They used the money from the sale to buy furniture, bedding, and appliances, and they hired a contractor for some additional renovation work.

Francis insisted his only goal in life was to ensure that Dara was happy and comfortable. Knowing that she was dissatisfied at her job, he offered her a position at his company. He handled all the bills, banking activities, and tax filing; this was a huge relief for Dara, who had always hated managing those responsibilities alone. He even made her a second account holder on his credit card. Dara was ecstatic. She'd never been with someone so eager to take care of her. It felt like everything was coming together: a new relationship, a new home, a new job. And after six months, getting married felt like the natural fulfillment of their deep, unique love.

As time went on, Dara came to realize that Francis was almost hyperaware of how much money she spent. He began accusing her of having poor skills with money management, claiming to be concerned about how her fiscal irresponsibility could impact them in the long run. He encouraged Dara to be more money conscious, offering to help her along the way—something Dara was initially very thankful for. She brought home all her receipts, everything from taking a yoga class, to lunches out with friends, to the weekly grocery shopping. Still unsatisfied, Francis proposed giving Dara a set amount of money each week, saying it would help her learn how to budget. Dara was less enthusiastic about this idea, but she agreed, taking his word for it that he was "smarter with money" than she was, despite his lavish spending style.

It wasn't long until spending money became an unbearably stressful situation for Dara. She no longer trusted herself to make any purchases independently; instead, she felt an increasing need to check in with Francis multiple times per day to ask permission to buy things, even items as trivial as an eyeshadow palette or a morning coffee. Strangely, the more she adhered to Francis's rules and deferred to him on all financial decisions, the more controlling Francis became. He would never just say yes or no, but instead scolded her for having such poor financial judgment. Rather than risk an argument with Francis, Dara began to avoid going out with friends or engaging in hobbies—anything that involved spending money. When her makeup was used up and her haircut had grown out, she felt too anxious and confused to do anything about it, even though Francis would often make remarks about how she was "letting her looks go." It never occurred to her to ask Francis why *he* felt okay about buying new golf clubs or flying to Mexico for a friend's bachelor party. She assumed he knew which expenses were appropriate or not, while she felt too incompetent to even ask questions.

What type of abuse is most prominent in this scenario?

____

What specific behaviors led you to this conclusion?

____

____

____

Anthony and Eileen

Growing up, Anthony had a close relationship with his mother, Eileen; they often called themselves "the dynamic duo." Eileen was known to be immensely proud of her son, loving nothing more than to brag about all his accomplishments to family and friends. But when Anthony started high school, their relationship started to shift. Eileen started picking arguments over seemingly trivial things, excluding herself from important family events, and arbitrarily giving Anthony the silent treatment. All of this left Anthony feeling hurt and wondering what he had done to upset her.

The closer Anthony got to adulthood—graduating from high school, entering college, finding an internship in his preferred field, and finding a significant other—the more tumultuous his relationship with his mother became.

One day, Anthony came home with exciting news: He and his girlfriend were engaged and planning to move across the country to California for her job. What should have been met with smiles and cries of celebration was met with anger from Eileen. She began to berate Anthony, calling him selfish and inconsiderate. After she'd taken care of him his entire life, how could he just abandon her to care for herself? She wailed at him, "No good son does this to their mother! After everything I've done for you!" She insisted that if he really cared about her, he would never let "another woman" take him away from her.

What type of abuse is most prominent in this scenario?

____

What specific behaviors led you to this conclusion?

____

____

____

Eleanor and Doug

After years of trying to make her marriage work, Eleanor had finally taken steps to initiate a divorce. She knew this would never be an amicable divorce and was prepared for a lengthy, contentious battle. Doug was unwilling to agree with anything Eleanor set forth, no matter how hard she tried to make it equitable. Most distressing for Eleanor was Doug's demand for full custody of their two kids. After Doug claimed that Eleanor was mentally unstable and unfit as a parent, the judge ordered Eleanor to undergo a psychological evaluation as well as a vocational evaluation to determine her current earning potential and ability to return to work. When their first child was born 17 years ago, Doug had insisted Eleanor be their children's full-time caregiver. Now, she had to scramble to find a job, accepting a part-time position.

The constant barrage of attorney meetings, court appearances, evaluations, and ongoing reviews of legal documents resulted in a slew of missed workdays and a mountain of legal fees; as a result, Eleanor maxed out her credit cards, drained her savings, and prematurely withdrew money from her 401(k), falling deeply into debt. But even after she expressed these financial concerns to Doug, he continued to present frivolous claims and deliberately delay hearings. At risk of losing her home and her new job, both of which could negatively influence the court's custody decision, Eleanor felt she had no other option than to give in to Doug's demands in the hopes that it would end this legal nightmare.

What type of abuse is most prominent in this scenario?

____

What specific behaviors led you to this conclusion?

____

____

____

Toxic Behavior Patterns or Narcissistic Abuse?

The previous sections may have looked familiar if you're in a relationship with a narcissist. However, there are many toxic relationship dynamics that appear to *mimic* narcissistic abuse on the surface. Underneath, the reasons for these behaviors are inherently different from those of a narcissist. This is another downside of the overabundance of nonclinical content on narcissism and narcissistic abuse: leading more people to misinterpret others' actions and misjudge their own personal relationships.

As we touched on earlier in the chapter, people can display interpersonally toxic behavior without meeting the diagnostic qualification of NPD. Sometimes a person's behavior patterns appear narcissistic, but the underlying function of the behavior is not to control, gain power, or harm the other person. Rather, their actions are the result of long-standing, unhealthy, learned behaviors from their upbringing. But before pinpointing the purpose of an individual's behaviors, we must first consider the main distinctions between unhealthy relationship patterns and narcissistic abuse.

Intention

You may assume that the woman in your office who interrupts conversations to talk about herself, starts arguments over insignificant issues, and becomes overly defensive when challenged might be a narcissist, but she also might have a long-standing history of feeling unheard and invisible growing up and being constantly criticized by her parents over trivial things. Her intention is not to hurt, manipulate, and control others, but rather to simply be seen and valued. She tries so hard to not interject herself into conversations and only yelled at a coworker for what she perceived as an attack on her intelligence and competency.

The guy you dated for six weeks who suddenly stopped returning your calls could potentially be a narcissist; he also might have learned from an early age that people who are supposed to love you will leave you. So, he protects himself from vulnerable feelings by withdrawing from or sabotaging relationships when they get too intimate. His intention is not control; it is self-protection. He is always left with intense feelings of shame and embarrassment after abruptly ending his relationships. He doesn't want to hurt you, but the fear of abandonment is just too overwhelming.

While these types of behavior are still unhealthy, their intent isn't about punishing, controlling, or manipulating other people. Rather, it is a long-established pattern that is familiar and safe, something they can rely on in emotionally stressful situations despite the often negative consequences. A narcissist's intention, on the other hand, is to obtain power and control however they need to—even if it means causing harm to others.

Capacity for Empathy and Remorse

Another factor that helps distinguish true narcissists from people with deep-rooted interpersonal difficulties is what they do when information about their behavior is brought to their attention. Most people feel some measure of remorse when they learn that another person was hurt by what they did or said. A narcissist, however, is not only aware of the pain they are causing but will often respond with indifference or even take pleasure in knowing they have hurt someone.

Imagine that you have a pattern of interpreting constructive feedback as a personal attack on your character. You shut down emotionally and withdraw from the person who provided the feedback. If a loved one brought this to your attention, gently telling you that sometimes your behavior hurts those who care about you most, you may well become defensive at first, but the bigger question is how you respond after you've had time to think it over.

Does it make you sad to hear how your behavior is responsible for hurting the ones you love? Do you take accountability for your actions? Most importantly, are you willing and motivated to make changes despite the difficult road that may lie ahead?

If your response to these questions was yes, then it may be that your difficulty receiving feedback is the result of a learned behavior pattern. It may significantly impact your relationships, but with awareness, accountability, and consistent effort, it can be changed over time.

An authentic empathetic response, along with a willingness to change and take accountability for the harm caused by their behavior, is in direct contrast to the core characteristics of someone with NPD. A true narcissist would most likely respond to the previous questions with answers like "This is who I am—they can either accept it or not," or "If they are hurt by my behavior, that's their problem. They shouldn't have gotten me so angry."

It's worth noting that some narcissists may successfully act remorseful and even appear as if they are making efforts to truly change their behaviors. But these efforts are typically short-lived, lasting only as long as they serve the narcissist's own interests. For example, they may tell you they take full responsibility for their actions and make promises to change, just to manipulate you back into the relationship. Or they may claim they want help for their drug addiction and agree to enter a substance abuse treatment program, but only because they're trying to avoid losing their job or looking bad in the community. The narcissist's effort to change their behavior is not because they believe they need to, but because of what they stand to gain from the change. Once they get what they need, they will ultimately resort back to their old patterns.

It's Not the What, It's the Why

A crucial point that is often missed in the popular understanding of narcissism and narcissistic abuse is the function of the narcissist's behavior. In other words, what really marks a narcissist isn't *what* they do, but *why* they do it. The "what" is simply surface-level words and actions the narcissist uses to distract and destabilize you in the moment. By throwing you off balance, confusing you, and creating self-doubt, you become easier to control. They'll use any tactics to achieve this goal, from excessive compliments and displays of attentive care to the silent treatment, rage, baseless accusations, and violent intimidation.

If you're in a relationship with someone whom you suspect of being a narcissist, ask yourself the following question: *Why* is *this* person demonstrating *this* specific behavior, in *this* specific manner, at *this* exact time and place?

ACT Concept

Why Versus What

ACT strategies help you stop reacting to the surface details of the narcissist's behaviors and words and instead ask yourself, "What is the function of their behavior? What are they trying to get from me in this moment?" Responding based on the *why* means targeting their need for control rather than the superficial manner they used to achieve it. It's important to understand that a response to the *why* should never be to offer them empathy or support. Rather, you must put yourself in the driver's seat when deciding what your next steps should be.

For example, suppose your partner starts a random argument with you about how you are dismissive of their feelings, and they storm out of the house, disappearing for the rest of the day. While this may seem to have occurred out of the blue, for a narcissist, there is *always* a motive. Ask yourself, *why* now? *Why* this? In this instance, you have a friend's surprise birthday party that evening. The narcissist's behavior has nothing to do with you being dismissive of their feelings, and everything to do with wanting to control your emotions, thoughts, and behaviors to ruin your evening with friends.

Or maybe they took your car without asking and did not fill up the tank with gas. The next morning as you are leaving for work, you realize that you now need to stop for gas, which will make you late for an important meeting about your promotion. You may be tempted to argue with them about being irresponsible with your car, but the underlying reason, or *why,* for their actions was to deliberately cause you chaos by sabotaging your meeting.

Focusing on *why* over *what* can provide insight into whether a person's behaviors are potentially the result of learned unhealthy coping skills or part of an agenda to gain wholesale power and control over you. While on the surface the behaviors may appear the same, the crucial difference lies in the behavior's function.

We will explore this concept more in chapter 3, when we dive deeper into patterns of interpersonal behavior.

The Impact of Narcissistic Abuse on Your Health

If you are not being physically harmed, it can be easy to dismiss an individual's behavior as not abusive. You may think that if you just learn how to deal with it better or change your responses, you can figure out a way to live with it. This notion that abuse only exists if there is visible evidence is a dangerous myth that often keeps people stuck in narcissistic abusive relationships. You buy into the misconception that if there are no physical bruises, then it must mean you are too sensitive or overreactive.

But it is this silent, coercive controlling behavior that, over time, erodes your self-identity and takes a devastating toll on both your body and mind.

Cognitive Function

Long-term narcissistic abuse and other forms of coercive control not only create considerable psychological trauma, but they also lead to living in a chronic state of fight or flight; combined with years of gaslighting and abuse, this actually alters the wiring of your brain, which has devastating consequences for cognitive function. Many people will describe living in a "fog" that makes it nearly impossible to concentrate on even the most routine tasks. The ability to pay attention and retain information when simply watching TV, reading a book, or engaging in a brief conversation is affected. Impaired short-term memory is the most reported cognitive difficulty of narcissistic abuse survivors, but it is not uncommon for survivors to also report increased clumsiness and even higher incidence of car accidents due to distracted thinking.

Many people also present with tremendous difficulty making even the smallest of decisions. Their attention, concentration, and ability to retain information is compromised by their state of fogginess and confusion. This, along with years of gaslighting, results in a loss of confidence in their decision-making abilities, creating increased dependency on the narcissist to make decisions on their behalf. They also have a significant amount of self-doubt in their ability to accurately perceive the reality of the world around them, making even the smallest decision feel scary and overwhelming.

Mental Health

The social isolation and loss of self-identity and self-worth puts survivors of narcissistic abuse at risk of developing mood disorders, posttraumatic stress disorder (PTSD), eating disorders, substance abuse, and suicide risk. Years of narcissistic abuse can lead to something known as *complex posttraumatic stress disorder* (C-PTSD). While C-PTSD is not recognized in the *DSM*, it is highly prevalent in survivors of narcissistic abuse in relationships of all kinds. Unlike PTSD, which is a response to a singular traumatic event (e.g., assault, car accident, natural disaster), C-PTSD develops from prolonged and repeated interpersonal trauma. Symptoms of C-PTSD can include extreme emotional dysregulation, overwhelming feelings of shame and guilt, and long-standing physical conditions, such as stomach issues, fatigue, and chronic pain.

Another type of trauma to arise out of narcissistic abuse is something known as *betrayal trauma*. This can occur within any relationship where one person is highly dependent upon the other for psychological, emotional, or financial support, such as a parent-child dynamic or an intimate relationship. My patients often experience absolute shock in learning that someone they are heavily reliant on is not who they believed them to be; this life-changing violation of trust can be traumatizing, leaving them feeling violated, confused, and grief-stricken. Their ability to trust is shattered, as is their confidence in accurately perceiving the intentions of others—both of which result in increased social isolation, hopelessness, and depression.

Physical Health

Anxiety itself is a naturally occurring emotion. It gives us information about the world around us, can increase motivation levels, and helps to keep us safe. For example, if someone is chasing you down the street, your brain acknowledges you're in danger and subsequently sends a message to the rest of your body to respond accordingly. When your brain perceives your environment to be dangerous, your fight-or-flight response is triggered so that you can effectively manage the dangerous situation. When this occurs, you may experience physical symptoms, such as a racing heart, shortness of breath, or sweating. These symptoms and sensations can feel awful and scary, but they are not dangerous. Rather, they keep you safe from harm.

While the human brain and body are well equipped to deal with acute and sudden threats, prolonged stress responses can have detrimental consequences on our mental, cognitive, and physical health. When we are stressed, overwhelmed, or anxious, our body releases a hormone known as cortisol. In short bursts, cortisol aids us in regulating our body's response to stress. This includes regulation of blood pressure and metabolism as well as a reduction of inflammation.

Those in narcissistic abusive relationships will often present with elevated cortisol levels. The intermittent reinforcement of the abusive dynamic causes a tremendous amount of confusion, uncertainty, depression, and anxiety. Their brains are constantly on high alert, routinely scanning their environment for imminent threats, even when one is not immediately present. The constant fear and hypervigilance send the body into a chronic state of fight or flight, which ultimately has deteriorating effects on physical health. Examples of health issues frequently seen in survivors of narcissistic abuse include autoimmune diseases, heart disease, chronic pain, high blood pressure, digestive issues, migraines, memory problems, hair loss, skin rashes, sleep difficulties, joint pain, and even increased risks of heart disease and cancer.

Conclusion

Narcissistic abuse goes beyond hurtful or toxic behaviors. It is a complex and uniquely insidious form of abuse that infiltrates your core sense of self, fostering a deep emotional and psychological dependency that has devastating consequences for your mental, cognitive, and physical health.

Recognizing this abuse for what it is—a calculated effort to strip you of your self-identity and agency solely to satisfy the narcissist's need for control and power—can be a devastating realization. It can feel like your world has been ripped out from under you. Many survivors become so accustomed to minimizing the abuser's behavior that their initial reaction is to blame themselves. The systemic devaluation of your self-worth may make you feel as though you were somehow deserving of the abuse.

Nevertheless, once you've seen the distinct blueprint of narcissistic abuse you can never unsee it. This clarity creates a crack in the narcissist's facade that will only continue to expand. Instead of feeling at the mercy of their volatile moods and arbitrary expectations, you'll begin to see patterns in their behavior that allow you to predict when, why, and how they'll react to different situations. This pattern-spotting has a liberating effect. It dawns on you that their abusive behavior is not, and never has been, about you. It's always been about *them*.

As your sense of clarity increases, it's imperative to get safe, accurate guidance about how to navigate your way out of the relationship. This is where the misinformation and half-truths on social media can be particularly harmful. Even well-meaning advice like "Hold your boundaries" and "Take back your power" can backfire when it doesn't account for the deep complexities of narcissistic abuse. The way in which you assert yourself and set boundaries within these relationships involves a highly nuanced behavioral approach that often gets lost within social media.

Social media influencers, friends, and even licensed mental health professionals can inadvertently lead you astray by focusing solely on empowerment, self-love, and self-worth without first implementing the necessary behavioral skills to effectively navigate triggers and separate yourself from the abuser's narrative. Without this specific practice, you're unknowingly setting yourself up to be pulled deeper into the abuse cycle.

Bottom line: If you've realized that you're in a relationship with a narcissist—whether it's an intimate partner, a parent, a friend, a boss, or a spiritual leader—you *must* be discerning about the informational sources you trust. After all, narcissistic abuse isn't just a source of emotional pain; it is also a very real and dangerous threat to your physical safety. Self-love can wait. Survival can't.

2

The Cycle of Narcissistic Abuse

The first light in the tunnel of narcissistic abuse comes when we recognize that it follows a specific behavioral blueprint. While the abuse does not manifest in a linear pattern, it is cyclical, marked by three distinct stages calculated to entangle the other person psychologically, emotionally, and often financially and legally, with the ultimate goal of eradicating their core self. The diagram on the next page shows this cycle.

Stage 1: Idealization (Love Bombing)

Narcissistic abusive relationships typically begin with a purposeful effort by the narcissist to capture your attention and trust. In the previous chapter, we touched on the fact that early in the relationship, abusers very often present a facade of concern, interest, helpfulness, and love. These behaviors, referred to as *love bombing,* may consist of over-the-top gifts like giant bouquets, fancy dinners, expensive jewelry, and surprise trips, or it may take the form of claiming to share the same interests, hobbies, even childhood experiences.

The Cycle of Narcissistic Abuse

Idealization Stage (Love Bombing)

- Relationship feels like a tidal wave of intense, sudden romance.
- You and your partner constantly communicate from the onset of the relationship.
- Your partner offers you gifts, trips, and lavish dates, even promising future marriage and family very early.
- Your partner is charming and overly complimentary; they put you on a pedestal.
- The relationship feels too good to be true; you might hear "You're my soulmate" or "I've been looking for you my entire life."

Devaluation Stage

- Once the narcissist has you hooked into the relationship, the love bombing stops and the fairytale is over; they become distant and pull away affection.
- The narcissist uses passive aggressiveness, silent treatments, and subtle putdowns to make you feel powerless and helpless.
- The narcissist will act loving at times, causing confusion and leaving you hoping and waiting for them to return to "normal," which will never occur.
- If you address these behaviors, the narcissist will deny them and accuse you of overreacting, being too sensitive, or lying.

Discard Stage

- Once you can no longer provide the narcissist with a sufficient supply, they will discard you.
- The narcissist wants you to feel unlovable and that no one will want you; verbal and physical abuse increase.
- The narcissist may stop contacting you suddenly and with no explanation.
- Because narcissists cannot be without supply, it is likely they have another relationship/partner in the wings; they may flaunt this new person on social media or to others.

Hoovering

- The narcissist tries everything to get you back into the cycle of abuse.
- This may look like random texts, promises to change, or even love-bombing behaviors.
- They may also cause unnecessary drama to make you upset or scared.

Love bombing is a tactic the narcissist leans heavily on when they are beginning to draw you in, presenting themself as highly attentive, dotingly affectionate, overly helpful, and heavily invested in your interests. Many of my clients describe this stage as feeling as if they got hit by a tidal wave. The connection does not progress organically or at a normal pace; rather, it comes on quickly and intensely. You are caught up in an immediate whirlwind. This fast-paced romance is not by chance—it is part of the narcissist's plan to sweep you off your feet so quickly that you have little time or desire to consider how unusual (and potentially unhealthy) it is for a relationship to move forward in such a brief period of time. They will be in constant contact with you, frequently calling and texting sentimental messages throughout your day. They will mirror your interests so that the two of you seem increasingly compatible, and appear deeply sympathetic toward your vulnerabilities and fears. The narcissist's goal in these actions is to make you feel incredibly special, so that you drop your guard and reveal the most intimate parts of yourself—only for them to weaponize these vulnerabilities against you later.

Not long after the initial meeting, they will begin to express a constant desire to see you. This typically results in *cluster dates*—spending several days in a row together without breaks. While this seems like the sincere efforts of someone who genuinely loves spending time with you, the escalated pacing and intensity are signs of a manufactured closeness intended to create a false sense of trust and safety. This is one way that the narcissist begins the gradual process of isolating you from other people whom you trust and depend on for support.

The narcissist will reinforce the illusion of this perfect connection by referring to you as their soulmate, perhaps telling you this was meant to be or that they fell in love with you at first sight. It isn't uncommon during the love-bombing phase to hear statements like "You are the only one who truly gets me," "You're my soulmate," "I've never met anyone like you before in my life," or "I don't know how I ever lived without you." They frequently push an "us against the world" narrative, which can seem romantic at face value but has an ulterior motive. You may misperceive this instant closeness as a unique connection, while the narcissist is gathering information about your vulnerabilities to control you in the future. They're not talking about the two of you facing challenges as a team; they're telling you that the relationship with them is the only relationship you can (or should) trust.

Early in the relationship, even as soon as the first date, the narcissist will also quickly escalate your conversations into deep talks about your long-term plans with each other, making grand predictions and false promises. This tactic, known as *future faking,* creates a false sense of security in the relationship and builds hope for a deeply fulfilling "happily ever after" scenario. Future-oriented promises like naming your future children, moving in together, or looking at engagement rings are often used early in the relationship to build your emotional investment in the relationship. Future faking is also used intermittently throughout the entire relationship to keep you tethered by the hope that the abuse will stop, they will seek help, and things will eventually get better.

Initial love-bombing behaviors may include a combination of the following:

- Being with each other for days at a time
- Talking on the phone or texting for hours daily
- Receiving gifts that are disproportionate to what one would expect early on (e.g., expensive jewelry, vacations)
- Talks of marriage and having kids specifically with you
- Having deep conversations about extremely intimate life details and vulnerabilities

- Referring to you as their soulmate and expressing a feeling of having known you their entire life
- Making future promises that are grand in nature
- Bringing you around family and friends after only a few meetings
- Offering to pay expenses (e.g., mortgage, car lease)
- Offering to help with household tasks and daily responsibilities (e.g., painting your house, babysitting your kids)

Keep in mind that one or two of these behaviors occurring early in the relationship does not mean you are being love bombed. Love bombing is a chronic pattern of manipulative behavior used to solidify reliance on the narcissist, all while framing their actions as genuine, helpful, and out of genuine love.

For my patients who are questioning if what they are experiencing is love bombing, I give them a small dating experiment to conduct. Let's say you've been dating someone for only three weeks, but it is moving extremely fast. The next morning after your most recent date, they text you asking if you would like to come over and watch a movie. Despite having spent every day together for the past five days, you still *really* want to see them. However, this time you decline the invitation, politely saying that you need to take care of something at home but are excited to see them tomorrow! While this may seem like an innocent response, to a narcissist it can be a form of rejection and a loss of control over the relationship. A healthy partner, even if disappointed, would respect your boundary, stating, "I understand. I will see you tomorrow! Can't wait." However, a narcissist would be more likely to respond in one of the following ways: They may stop responding to you completely, making you feel as if you've done something wrong. They may suddenly express that they don't think the relationship is working, leaving you confused. They may ignore your boundary by showing up at your house uninvited with flowers, offering to help you with your household chores, or by continuing to contact you throughout the day and making it difficult for you to get things done. Or they may respond appropriately to your boundary, only to hold it against you later on in the relationship as evidence for their claim that you are "selfish" and "only care about yourself."

It's easy to understand how someone can get pulled into these types of relationships. It's a rare thing to feel special, chosen, and deeply understood and loved. The intense, constant attention and the feeling of a powerful emotional bond are so captivating, it feels like you've hit the relationship jackpot—a stark contrast to what many people experience in today's dating world, where mixed signals and shallow, inconsistent connections have become the norm. Thus, when you meet someone who appears to provide intense attention, clarity, and connection, it can feel like you've finally found everything you've been looking for.

While instant connections and magnetic attractions can certainly happen, they are often rooted in surface-level criteria like physical appearance, conversation style, and sexual chemistry, with limited personal information. For these early connections to develop into something truly healthy and lasting, the relationship needs to evolve naturally over time. Real connection is built on shared experiences. How does the person show up over the long term? How do they manage conflict? How do they process difficult feelings and experiences? Are they emotionally present? Are they supportive of your interests and goals? These are personal characteristics that take time to observe and learn. When you allow space and time for a relationship to organically unfold, your connection will be grounded in authenticity instead of on surface-level illusions and idealized fantasies. When a connection feels like a tidal wave knocking you off your feet, so fast and furious that it feels too good to be true, that's because it usually is.

While the behaviors in this first stage don't appear how most people would traditionally define abusive, they aren't genuine. Rather, they are the manipulative tactics that lay the groundwork for the narcissist's abusive cycle. The purpose of the intensity and speed in which the connection is formed is to overwhelm you with heightened emotions to the point that you have no chance to evaluate the relationship reasonably. It's also intended to make you feel, for lack of a better word, addicted to their attention. The flood of affection and connection acts like a chemical high—it's no wonder you want it all the time! Keep in mind that this dependency on them is *not* because you have low self-esteem or lack confidence. Rather, your brain has come to associate these emotional highs with trust, stability, and safety.

This is exactly where the narcissist intended you to be; this is the first stage of the abuse cycle.

Stage 2: Devaluation

It is often true within most relationships that a gradual shift occurs from a honeymoon phase to a more measured dynamic. In a narcissistic abusive relationship, this is not the case. Like the whirlwind romance of the idealization stage, the transition to this next stage typically comes without notice or rational explanation.

While every relationship may experience some bumps as both people attempt to navigate this new landscape, it's at this point that a narcissistic relationship makes a noticeable shift. Devaluation often begins with a shift in tone. The narcissist's words and behaviors, formerly doting, become tinged with passive aggression. They may make subtle digs about your appearance, interests, or intelligence, brushing them off as jokes or helpful feedback. This may sound like "Are you sure about that outfit? You look like you're trying too hard" or "You know you are terrible with numbers—just let me handle the finances." Their constant praise curdles into criticism and judgment, often masked as concern: "Something's up with you. You've been acting differently lately. Maybe you should see a therapist."

Therapy and Narcissism

It might seem odd that a narcissist would suggest therapy, given their constant efforts to disguise their true intentions and their fear of exposure. However, you would be surprised by how many survivors seek couples therapy at the suggestion of the narcissist. This may be within the context of false promises, with no intention of actually following through with therapy. Or the narcissist may use the therapy sessions as another opportunity to gaslight you into believing that the abuse isn't real or that you are the one who is abusive. This often occurs when you fear speaking the truth in the session and the narcissist manipulates the therapist into believing their narrative. Rarely, if ever, will a narcissist suggest therapy with the genuine intention of changing their behavior.

It is not uncommon for survivors to initially overlook these behaviors, especially coming on the tail of all the recent love-bombing: "Surely someone who treats me so well couldn't possibly mean *that*," "They must have had a bad day at work," "They would never purposely say something like that to me." While these slights may be overlooked, the subtle digs are serving a larger purpose. This is where the narcissist slowly begins the process of stripping away your self-identity and trust.

Depending on the specific dynamic, this stage can come about gradually or have a sudden onset, usually beginning in response to the narcissist's perception that their control and power has been threatened. As you naturally become more comfortable letting your true self emerge, the "real" you conflicts with the perfect idealized version the narcissist had created in their mind. They start perceiving benign mistakes, normal personality traits, and appropriate boundaries as deep character flaws. Seeing this now "less than perfect" person, the narcissist will respond with criticism. This is *not* because you did anything wrong, but because you are no longer the idealized version the narcissist seeks to control. It is at this moment that love bombing gives way to devaluation.

This behavior may then be amplified with sudden, seemingly random outbursts of frustration and anger, as well as intermittent silent treatments. The narcissist becomes increasingly accusatory over trivial things, deliberately provoking conflict, disconnection, and a sense of unease. They may suddenly start an argument over the way you parked your car in the driveway even though that's the way you've always parked. They may throw your phone against the wall because you came home five minutes late from work and didn't give them notice. They may control or cancel your plans through verbal manipulation, guilt, or physical intimidation.

Typically, these outbursts are followed by treating you with complete indifference, by sweeping the incident under the rug or denying your perception of events. This is where we begin to see an escalation of gaslighting and other psychological abuse tactics.

From time to time, the narcissist may also return to love-bombing tactics, although with less intensity and frequency than in the idealization stage. This diluted version of love bombing, referred to as *breadcrumbing,* is another common tactic in the narcissistic abuse playbook. It can include vague apologies, affectionate behaviors, gifts, and promises that next time things will be different. Its purpose is to instill just enough hope that you remain psychologically dependent, despite the narcissist having no intention of changing.

While the groundwork is laid throughout the idealization stage, it is in the devaluation period when the narcissist escalates their campaign to isolate you from your support system. Without outside people to help validate your experiences, you become increasingly dependent on the narcissist to define what is real. Narcissists create social isolation in several ways. It usually starts by speaking negatively to you about your family, your friends, your boss, and even your therapist—anyone whom the narcissist sees as posing a threat to their control, their narrative, and their public image. They plant seeds of distrust in your support system by hinting that these individuals do not have your best interests in mind, even that they are jealous of your relationship with the narcissist. These efforts may happen in the context of arguments, but they can just as easily be couched in times of affection (e.g., "No one will ever love you like I do") or be presented as casual observations ("Honestly, I don't understand how you consider her your best friend. I didn't trust her the moment I met her"). If the narcissist senses any possibility of a rift between you and someone close to you, they will leverage it to their benefit ("Don't worry about what he says—he is just jealous of what we have and wants to sabotage us"). If they learn or even sense that you're confiding in other people, they may use guilt ("I can't believe you'd talk about our private life to other people") or outrage ("If you ever talk behind my back again, it's over!") to silence you.

Devaluation comments may sound like the following:

- "You don't need all that clown makeup on your face. You look better without it."
- "I know she's your best friend, but there is something about her I just don't trust."
- "You spend money on such silly things. I'll help you manage your money better."
- "Do you always let your parents' opinions influence you this much?"

- "Are you really going to eat all that food?"
- "Do you think you would even be able to handle a promotion? You're so stressed as it is!"
- "I'll book the vacation. Knowing you, you'll send us to the wrong city!"

The devaluation stage is all about destabilizing you to make you easier to control. The narcissist's erratic shifts from warmth and affection to coldness and cruelty keep you confused and on edge, never knowing if your initial loving connection will be restored. Moving from such an encompassing state of trust and attachment to this new state of unpredictability and uncertainty is deeply destabilizing to your nervous system. As a result, your body kicks into an anxious overdrive, desperately trying to get that original connection back. This may look like overapologizing when you've done nothing wrong, blaming your own actions as the cause of their abusive behavior, or suppressing your own needs to keep peace and manage the narcissist's moods. You may sense that something is deeply wrong, but your awareness is often overridden by the confusion they create through intermittent displays of love and concern amid the manipulation, gaslighting, and intimidation. This confusion keeps you psychologically intertwined with the narcissist even as you begin to fear that the person you fell for is disappearing. The fact is that they never existed in the first place.

Stage 3: Discard

The discard stage comes when the narcissist's carefully crafted dynamic starts to crack. This may happen because they sense control and power slipping away (e.g., if you begin setting strict boundaries or call out their true character), but more often, it's because they feel that you are of no further value to them. Remember, narcissists need a constant supply to maintain their self-image and worth. When they are no longer satisfied with the level of control, admiration, and power they are receiving, they disconnect from the relationship.

In the discard phase, the narcissist vacillates between being cold and aloof to being verbally hostile and even physically or sexually violent. They may suddenly break up with you, and the very next day, post pictures of themself with their new partner on social media. They may go completely silent, disappearing for days or weeks without explanation. While it may feel as if this behavior comes out of the blue, the discard is rarely sudden. In fact, the discard process began long before the narcissist's final act. In their mind, they have already devalued you; you no longer reflect the idealized version they have of you. They have already emotionally checked out of the relationship, and more than likely, have acquired a replacement supply. Losing access to, or needing more, narcissistic supply brings out their true nature: extreme rage, cold withdrawal, or an escalation of manipulative and abusive behaviors to regain control in the relationship. Although you are likely aware the relationship is not healthy, the discard may feel abrupt and jarring. It is yet another tactic used to destabilize you.

You might think that such behavior would be incontestable evidence to the narcissist that their behavior is reflective of an abusive pattern. Unfortunately, this never works the way it should. Any attempt to show the narcissist that what they're doing is wrong, or simply that the relationship is unhealthy, will be met with either denial, rage, or blame-shifting: "You're the reason I got so angry and broke your phone," "I wouldn't have cheated if you'd been a good partner," "You're always nagging and picking at me until I snap." They will allege that you are hypersensitive or even paranoid: "Everyone thinks you're nuts," "Everyone seems to see this but you," "Everyone warned me about you."

After years of enduring the narcissist's abuse, you may reach a breaking point in response to what, on the surface, appears benign. For example, the narcissist may purposely "forget" to get the mail. While this may be irritating, it doesn't warrant a response of extreme anger or rage. However, for someone who has been repeatedly controlled and abused for extended periods of time, the purposeful act of not getting the mail, in culmination with all the other abusive acts, can be an emotional breaking point. The narcissist can then use your extremely heightened response to this seemingly "trivial" mistake as evidence that *they* are the healthy one in the relationship; it's you who is abusive. It is not uncommon for the narcissist to record your outbursts and share them out of context with your friends, family, or even coworkers. They frame it as genuine concern for your well-being and safety while conveniently omitting that their own ongoing abuse is what provoked your entirely valid response.

This behavior can be absolutely jarring. It leaves you not only emotionally devastated but also mentally exhausted. You may spend tons of emotional and cognitive energy trying to make sense of how someone who once adored you and made you feel so safe could be so cruel. You may endlessly replay scenarios in your head, fighting all the while against a feeling of unreality—is this really what happened, or are you in fact the crazy one?

Hoovering

It's important to understand that "discard" doesn't necessarily mean a permanent end of the relationship in the narcissist's mind. This is because a narcissist views people as their property—an object that fulfills a specific need for them. They may never completely "let go." At any point after a discard, if the narcissist feels that need again, they may attempt to reestablish contact with the person who used to fulfill it and manipulate them back into the abusive relationship. These post-discard reconnection tactics are known as *hoovering*.

Hoovering often takes on many forms. It can present as intermittent love bombing. The narcissist may buy you something you've always wanted, send you unexpected compliments, or do a huge favor that you didn't ask for. After months or even years apart, they may write you a heartfelt letter of apology or show up with a repentant attitude, saying that they miss you, they need you in their life, they want to rekindle the relationship, or they simply want to meet with you to "clear the air." They may claim they have really been working on themself and feel tremendous guilt for how they treated you in the relationship. They may even ask you to attend a therapy session with them or demonstrate changed behavior for a brief period of time. These are all tactics designed to exploit your hope and dismantle your boundaries.

It's vital to understand that this reconnection is *not* because of any real feeling on the narcissist's part, much less a genuine change. The only reason they attempt to reconnect is because they want something from you. Perhaps they want to see if they still have access to your thoughts and feelings. Perhaps they have a specific need—sex, money, attention, admiration—that they haven't been successful in satisfying elsewhere. Sometimes, it's just for the sake of disrupting your peace, so that they can feel the thrill of power and control.

Another form of hoovering is leveraging pity and compassion. Rather than asking to rekindle the relationship, narcissists may present themselves as lost and helpless. They may say that they've lost everything—their friends, job, savings, home, health—and beg for your help, just for a little while. This is typically accompanied by expressions of deep humility, coupled with a return of lavish praise (e.g., "I know I don't deserve this from you, but you've always been the kindest person I know, and there's no one else I can turn to") and a tug on your tender feelings (e.g., "I know things didn't work out between us, but I've never forgotten how much we meant to each other back then"). These tactics are intended to make you feel bad for them or even obligated to help. However, once their need has been satisfied, they may cut you off completely without warning or explanation or, worse, they might use the opportunity to manipulate you back into the relationship.

Sometimes, hoovering is nothing more than an attempt to see if they can still get a reaction from you and disrupt your healing. Maybe they heard you're in another relationship or you recently took a new job. This can present as a seemingly random text with compromising photos or cruel statements like "You know no one else will ever want you," "You're nothing without me," or "Your kids are going to suffer because you're a terrible parent." They may feign illness to manipulate you into feeling guilt or launch a smear campaign against you with friends or coworkers, spreading around a narrative that attacks your character in hopes that you will expend your energy defending yourself against their lies. They could even decide after several months or years to suddenly threaten to take you back to court to revise child custody arrangements.

While hoovering may appear random and out of the blue, it is part of a specific timeline and cycle. Narcissists often initiate hoovering during another person's meaningful events, such as birthdays, graduations, anniversaries, or when they hear you are doing well and moving forward with your life. They choose such moments for a reason: They want to disrupt your happiness, stir up emotional chaos, and take you out of the present moment. Gaining access to your thoughts, emotions, and actions feeds them the supply they are seeking. Once the hoovering has served its purpose, and the narcissist's need has been met, they will resort back to their original patterns of behavior—until the need arises again.

Hoovering may look like the following:

- Immediately posting pictures on social media with their new partner at the same places you went together

- Calling you on the day of your mother's funeral to extend their condolences, or even showing up to the funeral
- Contacting your new boss to express false concern about your stability around students given your "drinking problem"
- Purposely showing up to the same workout class as you as if it was an accident
- Sending you an anniversary card despite not being together for two years
- Informing one of your family members that they "may" have cancer, and they have no one to turn to, in the hopes that the message will be relayed back to you

REFLECTION

Learning to recognize the various stages of the narcissistic abuse blueprint is a necessary step toward extricating yourself from the cycle. It helps you anticipate the narcissist's behaviors, rather than getting caught up in the gaslighting, manipulation, and emotional chaos those behaviors create. This awareness creates emotional, behavioral, and cognitive distance from the abuse, leading to greater clarity about the situation and more effective boundaries.

Each of the following case examples demonstrates a particular phase of the narcissistic abuse cycle. After reading each example, label it with the appropriate stage.

Cindy and Beau

When Cindy was only two years old, her mother passed away, leaving her to be raised by her father, Beau. Growing up, Cindy often walked on eggshells around her father, trying to avoid his seemingly random rage episodes. For years, it appeared that nothing she did could ever match her father's unrelenting standards. He would call her lazy, incompetent, stupid. But whenever Cindy accomplished something independent from her father, like receiving an A on an exam or scoring the winning goal in field hockey, he would deliberately undermine her sense of pride with belittling and condescending statements. He would often say things like "Calm down. It's ninth grade math, not Ivy League," or "Okay. You did one thing well. Let's not get carried away." These kinds of comments drained all of Cindy's ability to see any value in her achievements, giving her father control over how she determined her self-worth.

Cindy agonized for years about whether to cut ties with her father. Finally, after graduating from college, following decades of emotional and psychological abuse, she went no contact. At first, Beau claimed to be confused by her decision, denying that any abuse took place. He told her she was just seeking attention and making up stories for sympathy. He continued to avoid accountability, making himself out to be the victim in the relationship. When asked why he no longer spoke to his daughter, he would tell people she had "mental health issues" and that she was full of resentment because he had decided to move in with his longtime girlfriend.

Occasionally Beau would attempt to contact Cindy via email, but the message was always the same: Cindy was the one who needed help, and he would love to connect again once she was emotionally stable. Although it was difficult, Cindy continued to keep her distance from her father over the next 10 years.

Eventually, Cindy married and was about to give birth to her first child, and news of her impending due date reached her father. After not speaking to Cindy for close to 15 years, Beau called her on the due date leaving this voicemail: "I heard you are having my grandchild today. I hope you know how hurtful it is to be excluded from one of the most important days in my life. I hope you treat your child better than you treat me."

Which stage of the narcissistic abuse cycle does this scenario best demonstrate? Why?

____

____

____

Ashley and Martin

Ashley could not remember ending a first date with butterflies this intense. She had never felt so safe so quickly with someone—safe enough to share details of her abusive childhood, something she'd never shared with even her closest friends. But Martin made her feel so comfortable sharing her vulnerabilities; it turned out that he came from a very similar upbringing. Martin explained how his last wife was "crazy," left him for another man because he was having financial difficulties, and took full custody of his children. When Ashley expressed sympathy, he told her it helped so much to talk about it with someone like her. He told her that he knew right away that he could trust her, even though they just met—he said it felt as if he'd known her his whole life.

The similarities didn't end with their backgrounds. Ashley told Martin she loves to cook Peruvian food, which turned out to be his favorite food. She also talked about her love for animals and how her plan was to adopt a rescue dog in the next year. She couldn't believe it when he told her he had worked in an animal shelter for almost three years in college. Over dessert, they joked about marrying each other, how they would decorate their first home together, how many dogs they would adopt, and even what their future kids' names would be. As he walked her to her car after dinner, he said, "Ashley, I just know I'm going to marry you." Ashley lay awake in bed for hours, her head spinning with the whirlwind quality of her new romance.

The next week, Martin sent flowers to Ashley's work, thanking her for a wonderful night. He texted her sweet messages throughout the day and FaceTimed for hours before bed. He continued to confide in her about how deeply some of his prior girlfriends had hurt him—how they were overly critical, controlling, and verbally abusive. According to Martin, one ex still tried to contact him despite his best efforts to turn her away. Ashley instantly felt empathy for him, as she too had been taken advantage of in her prior relationships. She couldn't imagine how terrible these women must have been to hurt someone as kind and sensitive as Martin.

Which stage of the narcissistic abuse cycle does this scenario best demonstrate? Why?

____

____

____

Lisa and Derrek

Lisa, a fifth-grade elementary school teacher, loved her students and adored watching them learn and grow. During her eighth year of teaching, she was introduced to Derrek, the new assistant principal of the school. After many staff meetings and in-service lunches, Derrek and Lisa began spending time together outside of work; eventually, they began dating.

One day after work, Lisa went to the market for ingredients to surprise Derrek with his favorite homecooked meal. Lately, his mood had seemed distant and unavailable, but she figured he was stressed with work. When Derrek arrived at her house for dinner, he noticed the decorated table and well-prepared meal and instantly began laughing. "Oh Lisa," he said, "You can barely do basic addition, let alone figure out the fractions for a recipe! Are you trying to kill me with food poisoning? Anyway, I told you I was tired and just wanted to order pizza. Why don't you see if the neighbors want this? I love that you took time to do this for me, sweetie, but why don't you just stick to the prepared food aisle in the future?"

Despite Derrek's ongoing digs and passive-aggressive jokes, Lisa still cared very much for him, and they agreed to move in together. Soon after the move, however, Derrek began closely scrutinizing everything Lisa did. He would point out that the dishwasher was loaded wrong and complain about the way she folded his laundry. At first, his comments seemed like harmless suggestions, but over time they grew increasingly critical and accusatory. One day, Derrek came home from playing golf and immediately lost his temper, screaming at Lisa that the house smelled bad. He berated Lisa for over an hour about how she was incapable of doing anything in the house, and he couldn't believe he had agreed to move in with her. Eventually, Derrek locked himself in their bedroom for remainder of the night. He refused to let Lisa in the room, making her sleep on the couch. The next morning, Derrek acted as if nothing ever happened. Lisa was confused but didn't want to bring the issue up for fear of starting another argument before work. As he kissed Lisa goodbye, he reminded her to take better care of his home.

Which stage of the narcissistic abuse cycle does this scenario best demonstrate? Why?

____

____

____

Looking back at the case examples, have you experienced similar situations in your own relationships?

____

____

If you have experienced this in your own relationships, were you aware at the time that it may have been a form of abuse?

Where within the narcissistic abuse cycle did the behavior fall?

Why Breaking the Cycle Feels Impossible

The very features that make the narcissistic abuse cycle so complex are also what makes it so hard to find your way out, including self-doubt, fear, false hope, social isolation, and lack of support from those who do not see or understand the abuse. These factors also heavily impact your decision to leave or stay in the relationship, even long after you become aware of the behavior patterns.

The Danger of Breaking Up with a Narcissist

Breakups are always difficult, but a breakup with a narcissist is uniquely complex and can be dangerous. It often requires an actual escape plan given the degree of manipulation, and it carries a substantial risk of increased physical violence, particularly in the beginning. As explained in the stages of narcissistic abuse, the manipulation does not end when the relationship ends—in fact, it can often escalate into stalking behavior and physical violence. Leaving a narcissist isn't just a damaging blow to their ego; it's the ultimate loss of control and power, something they cannot accept. For this reason, leaving brings a significant risk of retaliation.

The abuse that continues after the relationship has ended is known as *post-separation abuse.* This can manifest in several ways, including false promises of change, legal abuse, intimidation, and escalation of physical violence—all of which are manipulation tactics to draw you back into the cycle. Regardless of its form, however, the purpose of post-separation abuse is the same: to regain control and power over you by targeting whatever they still have access to in your life (e.g., time, money, reputation, child custody).

When the narcissist can't exercise control over you directly, they will control how others perceive you through creating false narratives, spreading rumors, and divulging personal information and stories told in confidence. *Character assassination,* as this is known, is the narcissist's effort to undermine what's left of your social support and ruin your credibility regarding the abuse you've endured. Without a well-thought-out escape plan, you run the risk of being pulled back into the abuse.

The Addictive Quality of the Relationship

The relationship dynamics with a narcissist often mirror the cycle of addiction. The narcissist alternates between periods of manipulation, verbal and physical abuse, gaslighting, and other forms of coercive control, offset by episodes of affection, warmth, and watered-down love bombing. This unpredictability allows the narcissist to maintain control while keeping you stuck in an addictive loop of confusion, anxiety, and false hope that things will get better.

This unpredictable back-and-forth is known clinically as *intermittent reinforcement.* Simply put, this term refers to never knowing which of your behaviors will be met with affection and which will trigger the narcissist's silent treatment. On the occasions when your behavior is met with a desired outcome (e.g., a calm evening without arguing) your brain releases the neurotransmitter dopamine, a chemical that produces feelings of pleasure, relief, and satisfaction.

The biological purpose of dopamine is to motivate you to repeat rewarding behaviors—that's why dopamine floods your system when, for instance, you take your first bite of food after forgetting to eat all day or cross an item off a long to-do list. But your dopamine system can be hijacked by unhealthy behaviors too. People often talk about the dopamine effect of scrolling social media for hours or mindlessly eating junk food. The same effect occurs from anticipating the relief that comes when a narcissist shows a hint of being the person you once believed (and still hope) they are.

Intermittent reinforcement works on the same principle as addiction: The low moments cultivate a feeling of desperation and helplessness, which make the high moments feel even more rewarding, no matter how infrequent they may be. This cycle is notably similar to gambling behavior. While a gambler usually knows they have little control over the outcome of their bet, the anticipation of a potential win releases a hit of dopamine; the occasions when they do win bring a further spike of dopamine that results in a pleasurable "high." The pursuit of that pleasure spike motivates them to continue betting even when they know they should stop. The more money they lose, the more they crave that high again—although the high is never as satisfying as the first. The dynamics in a narcissistic relationship work much the same way: The more unpredictable the abuse, the more your brain chases the random and short-lived moments of kindness and affection. Over time, the brain begins to associate relief from pain with love, creating a powerful emotional and physiological attachment between you and the narcissist. This attachment, known as a *trauma bond*, is not rooted in genuine trust and intimacy, but in survival. Your nervous system has become conditioned to latch onto the small acts of positive attention as proof that the image of love the narcissist once portrayed is real and still present. Over time, this conditioning makes you feel powerless to walk away, even when you are aware of how harmful the relationship is.

My clients frequently report feeling trapped between the knowledge that this person is dangerous and toxic and the hope that the relationship will return to the fairytale romance it once was. Breaking a trauma bond requires untangling the chemical, emotional, and psychological ties that have been deliberately engineered by the narcissist to keep you in their abusive web.

Believing You Can Fix It

I've noticed an increasing volume of social media content asserting that narcissists are largely unaware of the harm their behaviors cause, and that their behaviors are the result of past relationship wounds or childhood traumas. Hearing these messages can exacerbate your tendency to believe that you can "fix" the person or the relationship if you just offer more understanding of their troubled past and have more empathy for the root cause of their actions. After you've endured years of abuse and mistreatment at the hands of someone you trust and love—and whose false promises you still want to believe—the idea of just walking away can feel as if all those years of care, effort, and hope are going to waste. The idea that things could change if you just tried a little harder or landed on the "right" approach is seductive; the thought of leaving the relationship, only to have the person you love find someone else and become the version of them you've always wanted is intolerable.

While it is true that many narcissists do come from chaotic, abusive, or neglectful backgrounds, their developmental histories don't absolve them of responsibility for the abuse they inflict on others. Furthermore, asking someone who has been psychologically, physically, and sexually abused to find more compassion for their abuser, who meanwhile takes no accountability and shows little remorse for their actions, is deeply misguided and often silences survivors. The truth is that narcissists *are* aware of the harm their behavior causes, and *they don't care*. They feel entitled to take any action necessary to obtain the admiration, power, and control they crave, and have little concern for those they hurt in the process.

What this ill-informed advice misses is that the narcissist understands how deeply you want to regain their affection and has no qualm about exploiting your compassion for them, your investment in the relationship, and your hope for change. The narcissist doesn't hesitate to weaponize your deepest human vulnerabilities against you—one moment they're promising you that they will change, the next moment they insist that leaving would be a reflection of *your* lack of commitment or your hard-heartedness for not giving them another chance. Taunted with accusations like "You don't care that this will tear our family apart," "You're making our children suffer," or "Clearly you're not willing to make this work," you hang on a little longer to avoid the self-blame, fear, and guilt of leaving while clinging to false hope that maybe this time they are telling the truth. The narcissist uses your empathy and hope against you, homing in on the idea that you are at fault for the abuse they inflict on you. You're likely to internalize this accusation, believing you are broken and unlovable and trying to "fix" yourself to prove your commitment and worth to the narcissist.

Nobody Believes You

All these obstacles to leaving a narcissistic relationship can feel more manageable if you have a supportive network—that is, people in your life who recognize the impact the relationship is having on you, who are more attuned to your mental and emotional state than the narcissist's charming facade or even your protestations, and who, at a bare minimum, will listen and believe you when you reach out for a lifeline. When you do reach out, it often begins as validation seeking for a growing sense that what you're experiencing is abuse, a confirmation that you are not, in fact, "going crazy."

Imagine trying to tell a friend that your partner, someone whom they have only ever seen behave kindly and affectionately with you, someone whom you have repeatedly declared to be your soulmate, locked you out of the bedroom because you didn't want to have sex. You'd like to think your friends would immediately rally around you, taking your side and helping you figure out what to do. In fact, most outsiders in this position meet the confession with tentative belief (e.g., "I can't believe he'd do that for real. Are you sure it wasn't just a joke?").

The problem is that the narcissist is so good at maintaining a charming facade to outsiders that your story can be met with ambivalence, doubt, and disbelief. In public, many narcissists are meticulous about portraying themselves as charming, attentive, and personable. Unlikely to engage in any noticeable abusive behavior, they will instead play the role of loving spouse, helpful friend, or caring parent. This deliberate facade is intended to gain admiration from those around them, and it is also a protective measure for their character and reputation, should stories of their abuse get out.

You may experience tremendous guilt when informing others about the abuse you experience because you feel as if you are exposing the narcissist to those who claim to know them well, such as family members. The narcissist's self-presentation in the community can make family, friends, and other outsiders skeptical of your story (e.g., "I've never seen Diana be anything other than attentive and loving to her son. She would never do anything to hurt him").

Likewise, narcissistic abuse has a way of pulling you back and forth. One day the narcissist's ice-cold stonewalling or outburst of rage may have you ready to walk out the door, and the very next day, they say or do just enough to rekindle your hope that they can change. It's no wonder that this can be confusing to outsiders (e.g., "Last month you said you weren't sure you could stay with him, then last week you post an anniversary photo, and now you're telling me he's a monster and you're afraid of him?"). Amid the confusion and self-doubt you already feel, how do you convince them that this is part of a larger pattern of abusive behavior?

Being misunderstood or doubted by others further corrodes not only your sense of safety and self-worth, but also your ability to trust your own perception. Therefore, it is neither necessary, nor healthy, for you to feel compelled to explain the abuse you've endured to everyone in your life, particularly to those who have been influenced by the narcissist's false narrative. This dynamic can create an additional layer of gaslighting, deepening your confusion, causing you to question the accuracy of your own perceptions, and potentially deterring you from confiding in others or leaving the relationship. For this reason, it is important that you maintain at least one safe and supportive person to turn to, whether that is a close friend, family member, therapist, or support group. It is helpful to have someone you can speak to about the abuse and someone who can listen with objectivity and compassion—and without judgment.

Conclusion

Understanding the cycle of narcissistic abuse doesn't make the pain they've caused you hurt any less, but it can help break the narcissist's hold over your emotions and sense of self-worth. After all, if the narcissist's behaviors are a calculated playbook for gaining power over you, that means they have nothing to do with who you are or what you've done.

There isn't any way for you to make them happy because happiness isn't what they want—*they want control.*

There's no question that it hurts to realize this about someone you've loved, cared for, or been invested in for many years. However, it also brings something you've been longing for: freedom. Freedom to stop anticipating their needs. Freedom to quit tailoring your behavior in the hopes of making them happy. Freedom to consider what life might be like if you could focus less on managing the narcissist's moods and more on other things that matter to you.

It might have been a long time since you've even thought about what matters to you, besides fighting for moments of calm and sanity amid the cycle of narcissistic abuse. Reconnecting with those core values is exactly what will give you strength to effectively navigate the narcissist's tactics, regain power and control over your life, and ultimately, recover your sense of self.

3

Seeing Patterns

Human beings are creatures of habit. We crave structure and routine. When your brain can predict what comes next, you are naturally more at ease; it gives you a feeling of stability in yourself, your surroundings, your behaviors, and your emotions. One way the brain creates this predictability is by identifying patterns within your environment. This helps you navigate different situations, anticipate the actions of others, and respond quickly and appropriately without draining your cognitive resources, freeing your brain to focus on everything else that truly requires your conscious effort.

For example, when you go out to dinner at a restaurant, you have a general idea of what the order of events will be: You'll be seated by the host and given menus, your drink order will be taken, followed shortly by your food order, then each course will be brought out, eaten, cleared, and so on until you pay the bill. If you've done this even a few times, it's unlikely you'll have any uncertainty about what to expect.

This same process applies to your interpersonal interactions, shaping your experiences and giving you a script that guides you in your relationship dynamics. Recognizing the behavioral patterns within your relationships prepares you to anticipate the actions of others. It also helps you to acknowledge your own response style and gives you insight into what feels triggering, familiar, and healthy.

Imagine that every Thanksgiving you attend family dinner at your aunt's house. Having been to her house for the last 15 Novembers, you can predict with a high degree of certainty the general course of the evening. For example, you know the order of events: drinks in the den while the kids play in the basement, appetizers passed around, dinner served buffet style in the dining room, and finally, dessert eaten on the porch. You are also familiar with the interpersonal behavior patterns of the guests, such as Uncle Tim's tendency to make passive-aggressive digs about your career, Grandmom Jane's perpetual comments on everyone's weight, and your cousin and his mother-in-law arguing about when he will give her a grandchild. Your familiarity with the guests helps you predict how Thanksgiving dinner is likely to play out. Because of this, you can focus your emotional and cognitive energy on setting necessary and effective boundaries: Calmly nod and walk away when Grandmom Jane comments on your weight, have a predetermined response to Uncle Tim's remarks about your career, and avoid sitting between your cousin and his mother-in-law at the table. Your familiarity with your family's patterns of behavior gives you a sense of control and empowerment, reducing the stress you would otherwise feel within the chaotic environment.

REFLECTION

Try one on your own. Pick something that has a familiar script for you. Maybe it is getting ready for work, a conversation with your boss, or a sporting event. In the space provided, flesh out your own personal script for a familiar scenario.

____

____

____

What makes interactions with a narcissist so difficult and distressing is that on the surface, their behaviors appear chaotic and unpredictable. Their responses seem to occur at random and are often disproportionate to what the situation calls for. For example, they might go into a rage because you didn't text them back within a timeframe that is acceptable to them, even though it didn't seem to bother them when you didn't text them yesterday. You may feel like you never know what version of the narcissist you're going to get. As a result, you walk on eggshells while trying desperately to predict and control the narcissist's mood and behaviors.

But narcissistic abuse is rarely random. As you learned in the previous chapter, it follows a very strategic, predictive cycle. The narcissist's seeming randomness is a deliberate part of this cycle, intended to throw people off balance so they will be easier to manipulate and control. This is why understanding the function behind a narcissist's behavior is essential for breaking free from their control. Recognizing the underlying *why* of their behavior (i.e., gaining control and power over how you act, think, and feel) gives you the clarity you need to establish effective boundaries against the *what* (i.e., the tactics they use to gain this control).

How Behavior Patterns Change

We typically develop our unique behavior patterns during childhood, in response to the behaviors of those who are most present and influential during our upbringing, particularly our caregivers. We might model their behaviors or develop adaptive responses to cope with their dysfunctional patterns.

For example, if you grew up in an environment that rewarded you for attending to others' needs at the expense of your own, you may have internalized the message that your needs were irrelevant, and that vocalizing or attending to them meant you were selfish or possibly even deserving of punishment. To survive this environment, you learned it was safest to neglect your needs and make others' needs your responsibility. If this narrative was routinely reinforced within your family dynamic, it could have a profound impact on your self-identity, your relationships, and the choices you make throughout your life.

As individuals transition out of childhood into adulthood, they may eventually come to realize that their long-standing patterns, which were once necessary for navigating their upbringing, no longer serve them well. When this realization occurs, one of three outcomes usually follows:

- They continue to engage in the same patterns that may have worked for them in childhood but are now maladaptive.
- They overcompensate for the ineffectiveness of their patterns by shifting to their extreme opposite.
- They find a healthy middle ground.

To continue with the previous example, if you learned to suppress your own needs, you may believe your selflessness is an act of kindness. Over time, however, you notice that most of your friendships feel one-sided and emotionally draining, and resentment starts to build. This gradual awareness may help you realize that constantly prioritizing others' needs while neglecting yourself has taken a toll on your mental and physical health. Some people use this realization to alter their behaviors, but others, even after this realization, choose to take no action toward changing their behavior. After all, changing lifelong patterns is difficult work, and despite their harm, habitual behaviors offer the illusion of safety and comfort. Many people understand that their patterns are unhealthy, yet the thought of changing them is petrifying. Giving up control and stepping away from what's comfortable feels far riskier because it's all they've ever known.

And so, our behavioral patterns can solidify into rigid, deeply ingrained ways of interacting. It's important to remember that these unhealthy patterns may form in two ways: (1) *directly modeling*—by repeating what was modeled by caretakers in childhood, or (2) *modeling the opposite behavior*—by severely overcorrecting in the opposite direction to avoid feeling powerless, unseen, or unsafe. Someone may genuinely believe these behaviors serve them well, perceiving them as necessary and advantageous even when they cause considerable damage to their life and the lives of those around them.

Returning to our previous example, the scenario where you've internalized the message that your needs are irrelevant, imagine that you've become emotionally exhausted from always meeting everyone else's needs. You feel taken advantage of and extremely resentful. To compensate for long-standing feelings of guilt, irrelevance, and shame, you commit to making your own needs the top priority and begin holding everyone around you to that same standard. You vow to never again tolerate feeling invisible, and you stop spending energy attending to the needs of others. Their needs fade into the background while yours become all that matter, and you do whatever is necessary going forward to ensure they are met first.

It is evident that either one of these extremes—continuing the behaviors that arose from the dysfunctional patterns of your upbringing or shifting to the complete opposite—can lead to unhealthy and maladaptive relationships. Both approaches operate from extremely rigid perspectives that do not adjust to different contexts. In other words, they lack *psychological flexibility*, a core component of ACT that means being fully aware in the moment and, based on what is needed in the present situation, maintaining or adjusting your behaviors according to your values.

It is important to note, however, that a narcissist will still see their actions as values-driven, yet their values are shaped by a distorted perception. They still lack psychological flexibility because they don't feel it's necessary to adjust their behavior to the situation. They are unfazed by the harm their actions cause others.

Old Patterns Versus Deliberate Coercion

Even in healthy relationships, old behavior patterns sometimes resurface out of habit or stress, without conscious intent to harm others. When the person becomes aware of the pain they've caused someone else, they typically assume accountability and make a deliberate effort to shift back into healthier patterns. A narcissist's behaviors, though also long-standing, are pervasive and deliberate, designed to manipulate, control, and satisfy their need for power.

To differentiate between resurfacing old patterns and deliberate coercive control, you can ask yourself the following questions:

1. What is the *why* of their behavior?
2. Do they take accountability when confronted?
3. Are they willing to change their behavior?

To illustrate this concept, imagine the following scenario: You arrive at work, and your superiors inform you that you've been awarded a promotion, one that you have been working hard for. Thrilled, you immediately call your partner to relay the good news.

You return home that evening, eager to celebrate your promotion with your partner. But shortly after your return, they start an argument with you seemingly out of nowhere. They accuse you of not having been attentive enough to their emotional needs following an argument they had with their parents. They call you a bad partner, a horrible listener, and an extremely selfish person. Completely taken off guard, you can't figure out what you said or did wrong. Instead of celebrating your promotion, your entire focus is now on them, their feelings, and what you can do to make the situation better.

1. What Is the Why of Their Behavior?

In our hypothetical scenario, if your partner was conditioned while growing up to believe that emotional expression is weak, and they were met with criticism and verbal abuse in the past whenever they expressed their feelings or sought help regulating them, they may have learned to keep their feelings to themself and to ruminate rather than regulate their emotions. This may lead them to becoming overwhelmed, resulting in an emotional outburst as a healthy form of release. Thus, the underlying function of their outburst is both to release their suppressed internal discomfort and to regain a sense of safety and control over their emotions by reverting to a familiar—though unhealthy—coping pattern. In this case, the function is *not* to minimize your accomplishments, gain control over your emotions, or reinforce any false narrative you've been conditioned to believe.

Let's say, however, that the function of their outburst was to gain back the power and control they thought was slipping away from them because of your recent success. Because your accomplishment deviates from their narrative, they engage in psychological manipulation and intimidation to eliminate any feelings of confidence and autonomy you may have. Whatever the reason, if the function is aimed solely at exploiting you or your emotions, or for the purpose of gaining power and control, it's not about a return to a familiar yet unhealthy long-standing coping pattern; it's coercive control.

2. Do They Take Accountability When Confronted?

The degree to which someone takes accountability is helpful when trying to understand the function of their behavior. Narcissists do not take accountability for their behavior, often shifting blame, deflecting, or gaslighting the other person. By contrast, people whose unhealthy behaviors stem from maladaptive coping rather than a need for power are more likely to take accountability, as the intent of their actions is not to purposely harm, manipulate, or control others. Remember, however, that while taking accountability for the role they play in hurting others is important, it in no way justifies or excuses their hurtful actions.

In the example scenario, you explain to your partner how this pattern is not only disruptive to them, but it also hurts you, and how tonight in particular, it tainted what should have been an occasion for celebrating your achievement.

Perhaps your partner hears you out, acknowledges their actions, demonstrates insight into why they did this, and expresses how sorry they are for ruining your special evening. They accept responsibility for the harm their behavior caused and redirect their attention back toward you and your accomplishment. Their expression of true understanding and remorse when confronted demonstrates a high level of accountability, suggesting that their behavior was not an attempt to control you.

On the other hand, being confronted can trigger an immediate defensive response. Someone might deflect, deny, or minimize your feelings, saying things like "What, like you're never in a bad mood?" or "Stop being so dramatic." Although this may feel manipulative, heightened emotions often reflect overwhelm and discomfort in the moment rather than the intention to manipulate, undermine, or gain control. The difference becomes clear after things settle down—if the person is willing to acknowledge the impact of their behavior and shows a willingness to change, their reaction was likely rooted in avoidance of their own internal discomfort.

However, when these types of reactions are persistent and serve to silence you, undermine your perception of events, or exploit your vulnerabilities, the lack of accountability is more likely to reflect a pattern of coercive control.

3. Are They Willing to Change Their Behavior?

Finally, we look at their willingness to change their unhealthy patterns of behavior.

Perhaps after calling you selfish, your partner leaves the house to go take a walk. Upon returning, they apologize for their hurtful behavior and agree to go to therapy with the goal of learning more adaptive emotion regulation skills and finally resolving this unhealthy pattern. Although you feel better having talked this through with your partner, you are still upset. You decide to postpone the celebration because the mood of the night has shifted. Your partner agrees to your wishes and continues to take accountability for their actions this evening. Eventually, they make good on their promise to go to therapy and work on their behaviors.

On the other hand, let's say your partner continues arguing and berating your character, saying you're a terrible partner and you only got the promotion because of your looks. This continues for hours, and it isn't until you capitulate, admitting they are right and apologizing for your selfishness, that your partner's behavior changes. The change is immediate and abrupt—as soon as you apologize, they present you with a dozen roses and reveal the celebratory meal they have waiting for you. In short, their anger and "hurt" dissipate as quickly as they appeared. But while they go on acting as if nothing happened, you are left feeling rattled and culpable, though you still aren't sure what you did wrong. You spend the next few hours in your own head, trying desperately to sort through the night's emotional upheaval—when you should be reveling in pride from your promotion.

In both examples, your partner has unhealthy behavior patterns that negatively impact your relationship. However, when we examine these behaviors through their function, we see that they are inherently different. One is based on long-standing patterns of bottling up emotions for fear of appearing weak, and the other is based on obtaining control and power over you through manipulation and coercion tactics that break down your confidence and strip you of your self-identity. Remember, even if your partner apologizes, appears to take accountability, and promises to change, it is essential to look at the historical context of the relationship, rather than one isolated event, when determining function. Do they have a history of faking accountability and making false promises of change? If so, it is more likely that their behavior reflects deliberate acts of coercive control rather than poor emotion regulation skills to release feelings of discomfort.

Identifying Patterns of Narcissistic Abuse

The slow and subtle onset of narcissistic abuse makes it extremely difficult to recognize early in the relationship. Masked by initial acts of affection, attention, and adoration, you may be unaware of the coercively controlling tactics until you are deeply immersed within the abuse cycle. It is quite common for survivors of narcissistic abuse not to fully comprehend the extent and severity of the abuse they've endured until after they have escaped it. But with more clarity surrounding specific patterns of a narcissistic individual, you may be able to pinpoint coercive behaviors more easily.

Step 1: Recognizing Patterns of Tactics

An effective way to cut through psychological chaos and regain clarity is to label the specific tactics used by the narcissist as they're happening. Taking this observer position creates psychological distance between you and the manipulation. Even if you don't notice the tactic the moment it happens, you can compare it to previous behaviors to gain a fuller picture of their manipulative patterns.

The following are some of the most common tactics narcissists use to obtain power, dominance, and control:

- **Baiting:** Intentionally triggering your emotions and exploiting your vulnerabilities to elicit an emotional reaction, which the narcissist will use as evidence that you are overreacting and to label you the "crazy" one.
- **Blame shifting:** Denying accountability and casting blame onto others for the consequences of their own actions.
- **Bread crumbing:** The intermittent showing of affection, attention, or false hope to keep a person emotionally invested in the relationship.
- **DARVO:** An acronym that stands for "deny, attack, reverse victim and offender," a manipulative tactic in which the narcissist denies any wrongdoing, blames you, and portrays themself as the victim while you are viewed as the offender.

- **Flying monkeys:** Enlisting friends, family, and coworkers to carry out the narcissist's manipulation and control tactics against you. Flying monkeys typically do not have an accurate understanding of the narcissist's true nature and believe they are simply being supportive.
- **Future faking:** Empty and often highly attractive promises made with the purpose of gaining your trust, connection, and emotional investment in the relationship.
- **Gaslighting:** Deliberately denying or distorting your reality with the goal of making you doubt your own perceptions, beliefs, memories, and judgment.
- **Hoovering:** Attempting to pull you back into the toxic cycle of abuse—this may appear loving (e.g., confessions of love, apologies, promises to change, contacting you on special dates and holidays) or menacing (e.g., accusations, insults, threats).
- **Isolation:** Deliberately creating division and distance between you and others close to you, such as family and friends, with the purpose of controlling your reality, making you reliant on the narcissist, and cutting off anyone who could validate your experience or challenge the abuse. They may do this by promoting an "us against the world" mentality, by insinuating that other people in your life are untrustworthy and jealous of your relationship, or by threatening to expose shameful secrets about you.
- **Love bombing:** Creating a false sense of security, intimacy, connection, obligation, or dependency via false promises, early and intense sharing of personal vulnerabilities (often falsely constructed), lavish gifts, and excessive admiration and attention.

- **Pathological lying:** Being compulsive and serially deceptive, lying to meet their own needs, avoiding accountability, and controlling your perception of reality.
- **Rage:** An intense reaction to perceived threats, criticism, and loss of control. This differs from typical anger in that it is disproportional to the actual context and aimed at punishing, controlling, intimidating, scaring, or manipulating you.
- **Silent treatment:** Withholding all interaction, affection, and communication from you, typically without warning or explanation.
- **Smear campaign:** Discrediting your character and credibility through spreading rumors, social media exploitation, sharing personal information, or disseminating private pictures, often with the goal of ensuring abuse claims will not be believed, preserving the narcissist's image, and painting the picture that you are unstable and abusive.
- **Triangulation:** Deliberately using a third party to destabilize your worth and control the narrative by withholding information or creating competition, confusion, and control, which gives the narcissist emotional leverage within the relationship.
- **Unsafe driving:** A form of control and punishment in which you are unable to safely escape a vehicle (e.g., reckless driving, speeding, driving while intoxicated, deliberately making you late, becoming violent, locking the doors).
- **Word salad:** Deliberately speaking in a nonsensical, circular, or confusing manner with the goal of destabilizing the other person, gaining assent, avoiding accountability, or derailing the conversation.

REFLECTION

Have you personally experienced any of those tactics in your own relationships? Briefly describe the context and what this looked like for you.

____

____

____

How did it make you feel?

____

____

____

What was the outcome?

____

____

____

Learning to recognize a narcissist's control tactics in the moment is empowering for survivors because it shifts their understanding of the abuse from confusion and self-blame to clarity and self-compassion. Instead of feeling that you are the cause of the abuse, you begin to see the narcissist's behavior as a predictable pattern with a singular purpose of gaining power and control over you and stripping you of your autonomy.

Step 2: Observing Patterns of Context

Given that a narcissist's primary aim is power and control, their coercive controlling behaviors often escalate at moments when they sense their control, influence, and dominance slipping away. This perceived loss frequently occurs when you take steps toward autonomy or when attention is directed away from them and toward you, toward someone you care about, or toward situations and experiences they are not a part of. The deeper threat, however, isn't just the absence of the spotlight; it's the loss of access to your internal world, particularly when external situations (e.g., a night out with friends, a phone call with family, going back to school for your college degree, spending the day with your child) do not reinforce the narrative the narcissist needs you to believe about yourself.

Keep in mind that the narcissist's need to access your internal world is not limited to evoking negative emotions; it also involves positioning themself as your sole source of positive feelings, such as validation, happiness, and comfort, increasing your dependency on them to define your reality and self-identity.

For example, imagine your childhood friends are throwing you a 40th birthday party—just six of you at a spa for the day. Upon arriving, you're told everyone's treatments have already been paid for and preselected by your narcissistic partner without your knowledge. While you understand your partner's true intentions, it is almost impossible to explain this to your friends. So, you put on a smile and nod as your friends rave about how wonderful and attentive your partner is. What they don't see, however, is that this incident is part of a long-standing pattern of control and manipulation masked as generosity. This isn't an act of kindness, but rather a manipulative tactic to position themself as the source of your happiness and the focal point of your special day.

Familiarizing yourself with the people, places, or situations that most often bring about observable coercive control tactics can help you remain emotionally grounded rather than confused, reactive, or blindsided. Now, this does not mean the abuse only exists in these visible moments. Narcissistic abuse is not a single action or isolated event; it is a persistent, pervasive lens through which the narcissist engages with the world around them.

The predictability of narcissistic abuse and coercive control becomes easier to understand when we frame it into two primary contexts: external and internal context.

Awareness of Your External Context

Your external context includes situations that can be observed outwardly or occur at a specific time, such as an event, a particular interaction, a meaningful moment, or an important date.

Special occasions such as birthdays, holidays, or other meaningful events are a frequent trigger for the narcissist's coercively controlling tactics; this is because such occasions typically direct attention away from the narcissist. It doesn't help that such occasions typically highlight your happiness, reinforce your connections and relationships with others, or celebrate your successes, all of which the narcissist views as threats to their narrative and grasp of control. (This is also why hoovering tends to occur around meaningful dates and events.)

Common External Triggers

- Holidays
- Birthdays
- Outings with friends
- Time for yourself (e.g., a hobby, working out)
- Anniversaries
- Promotions
- Graduations
- Plans with a specific start time (e.g., surprise party, dinner date)
- Work or project deadline
- Birth of a child
- Weddings
- Funerals

The following story illustrates how a narcissist might use an external context as an opportunity to manipulate and control someone.

You've noticed over the past several months that any time the topic of your career comes up, your new friend behaves in an odd manner, asking lots of questions about your position and your salary while at the same time making passive-aggressive comments about how you've become a workaholic. You've told them that these comments make you uncomfortable, only to have them respond, "Jeez, I'm just joking. Don't let your big important job take away your sense of humor."

One afternoon, after your boss assigns you a project with an immediate turnaround, you call this friend to cancel your dinner plans that evening. Your friend becomes angry that you had to reschedule. Later that night, they proceed to text you, suggesting new dates for dinner and repeatedly asking you to choose a time and a restaurant. When you don't respond immediately, their text messages become harsh and vindictive; they accuse you of being a selfish friend, especially after all the times they have been there for you. The messages become so frequent and outlandish that you can't focus on your project; eventually, you give in and call them back. But your friend keeps you on the phone long after you've committed yourself to a new dinner date, telling you how hurtful you've been and how they are the only one who puts effort into the friendship. Not once during the call do they acknowledge your work deadline. After a two-hour conversation, you are emotionally and physically drained, and you have no energy to finish your work. You email your boss for an extension, knowing they will be extremely frustrated with your last-minute request.

On its own, this incident may seem random, even justified—it's normal for a friend to be disappointed over canceled plans. But given this particular friend's pattern of behavior, it's worthwhile to take note and establish boundaries with them. Rather than hoping or waiting for your friend to change their behavior, you focus your attention on recognizing their unhealthy patterns and the "why" behind them. This gives you the clarity to choose an effective response—one that is not influenced by the heightened emotions of the context. You think back on all the other times when they've acted irrationally and passive-aggressively toward you, and you realize that it happens every time the topic of your job comes up. You decide to stop sharing with them about your career (even if they ask) and not to make plans with them during the work week. Actively changing how you interact with the narcissist can lead to increased feelings of self-control and empowerment while cutting off the supply that they are seeking from you.

REFLECTION

Record examples of triggering contexts within your relationship with a narcissist.

Triggering event, moment, or conversation:

____

____

Where were you? ____

Who were you with? ______________________________________

What was the specific context? ____________________________

____

____

What feelings and thoughts came up for you during the interaction?

____

____

____

What tactics were used by the narcissist?

____

____

____

What was the outcome?

____

____

____

Do you notice any patterns that emerge from the previous scenarios? This can include the people present, a particular type of event, a day of the week, a topic of conversation, and so on.

____

____

____

____

How do you see this pattern recognition helping you in future dynamics with a narcissist? What, if anything, would you do differently? Why?

____

____

____

____

Awareness of Your Internal Context

Your internal context includes the private experiences that occur within you, such as your personal perspectives, vulnerabilities, insecurities, fears, and deeply hidden wounds.

Sometimes, it may appear that the narcissist's abuse comes out of nowhere—in other words, you can't seem to articulate a specific event or situational trigger. In these instances, it is important to turn your attention toward your awareness of what is going on for you internally. Is there a particular vulnerability that you knowingly (or unknowingly) exposed to the narcissist? Narcissists thrive off others' perceived vulnerabilities and will exploit them to systematically break you down.

For instance, perhaps you have struggled with insecurities about your appearance for years. You never felt you fit in anywhere and never felt good enough. It is a core belief you have carried with you into adulthood.

You are taking your significant other to meet your parents for dinner. It will be the first time they are meeting anyone you've dated, and you haven't ever been this happy in a relationship, so it only seems natural to have them meet your parents. You arrive at the restaurant and head over to the table where your parents are waiting, walking hand in hand with your partner with a big smile on your face. Amid introductions, your mother immediately comments on how your hair looks. She loudly pronounces how upsetting it is that you "don't even care about yourself enough to look presentable in public." She proceeds to berate you for having so little respect for your parents that you'd show up to dinner looking this way, calling you "an embarrassment to the family."

In this example, there is no identifiable event or trigger—as this is your first time introducing a significant other to your mother. Instead, she seems to have been irrationally triggered by your obvious happiness in your relationship and your autonomy. To punish you for this, she proceeds to attack your innermost vulnerabilities—your insecurities about your appearance. Regardless of her reason, she deliberately goes for your emotional scar to punish you and break you down.

Understanding your internal context often requires deeper personal reflection than your external context. In this example, your mother triggered your core belief of *never being good enough*. Without conscious awareness that this trigger has been activated, your mind may interpret this as further evidence to confirm your belief. Your self-talk would likely spiral into all the ways you feel deficient—which is exactly how a narcissist gains access to your internal narrative and takes control over your self-identity to significantly influence your thoughts and behaviors. As a result, you may start an argument, shut down, or decide to cut dinner short.

Being aware of your internal context requires you to become highly attuned to your own internal triggers, beliefs, insecurities, and perceived flaws, along with the emotions and thoughts they bring up for you. The moment you grasp that your internal world is entirely yours, you take back a considerable amount of power from the narcissist. The narcissist can still impact your external circumstances (e.g., sabotaging an important introduction) or try to instill new insecurities, but they can no longer directly access how you feel or what you choose to believe inside your own mind. They are no longer the narrator of you; you are the narrator of you.

REFLECTION

What are some core beliefs you hold about yourself?

1. ______________________________
2. ______________________________
3. ______________________________

Create a summary of your internal narrative—the story your mind creates about you in relation to the world around you:

____

____

____

____

____

____

Considering your core beliefs and the internal narrative that results from them, answer the following questions:

1. Who is the original creator of this narrative?

   ____

2. Do you know why it was created?

   ____

3. Using a scale of 1–10 (with 10 being you believe it as 100 percent fact), how strongly did you believe this narrative growing up?

   ____

4. How was this narrative shared and reinforced by other family members?

____

____

____

5. At any point in your life, did you question this internal narrative? Why?

____

____

____

6. What would happen if you openly challenged this self-perception with those who reinforce it?

____

____

____

While it is important to understand how the core beliefs that make up your narrative came to be and why you hold on to them so tightly, it is even more important to recognize these narratives as they show up for you in the moment. In the previous example with your mother at the restaurant, if you were to pause in that moment and create space between yourself and your internal experience (e.g., the *I'm never good enough* belief), you could untangle from the thought, redirect your attention to the present moment, and respond to your mother in a way that is intentional (based on the why) rather than emotionally reactive (e.g., shutting down). This pause, which we will discuss later, is one of the most critical elements in forming boundaries and responses in a narcissistic abusive relationship.

Be aware that when you deny the narcissist entry into your internal world and limit their impact on your personal narrative, they may engage in manipulative tactics to pull you back into their cycle of abuse. One tactic is reverting to love-bombing behaviors, such as promising to change, suggesting you go to therapy together, or making other gestures in the name of a "fresh start" to your relationship. Another tactic is to hoover you back into the abuse cycle by starting a smear campaign against you, threatening to take custody of your children, or sending harassing text messages. Regardless of the specific tactic, the purpose is the same—to provoke a response.

REFLECTION

Consider one of your negative core beliefs. Then think of a few scenarios in which the narcissist purposely exploited this belief. In the space provided, describe each situation in a few sentences.

____

____

____

____

____

____

____

Use the following prompts to elaborate on your experiences:

Whom were you interacting with? ____________________

____

What was the topic of conversation? ______________________________

____

What were you doing at the time? ________________________________

____

Where were you? ____

____

What occurred immediately prior to the interaction?

____

____

____

How were you feeling prior to the interaction? During? After?

____

____

____

Do you notice any patterns or themes that emerge from these scenarios?

____

____

____

If you did notice patterns to what triggered your core belief, how does this observation change your perspective?

____

____

____

How do you see this pattern recognition helping you in future dynamics with a narcissist? What, if anything, would you do differently? Why?

____

____

____

Step 3: Identifying Patterns of Function

As we've discussed, it is not enough to look at the narcissist's behavior at face value; rarely are their words and actions aligned with their true motive. The primary function of a narcissist's behavior is to obtain control and power over you by whatever means necessary. The pattern of abusive control tactics shows the true motive of their behavior, helping you to react to the function instead of the observable, surface-level behaviors. Understanding the intent of their actions helps you create responses that are more strategic and grounded rather than emotionally driven.

REFLECTION

It's important to emphasize that you won't discover the function of a narcissist's behavior by asking them about their true intentions, much less through initiating a heart-to-heart where you share how their behavior makes you feel. There is no hope in engaging in a dialogue or argument, or convincing them to see your point of view. Instead, you must discover the function of their behavior and formulate boundaries in response. Once their efforts to manipulate, provoke, and confuse lose their effectiveness, you can start to reject their narrative and take back your power.

The following case examples demonstrate what happens when we respond to a narcissist's words and observable actions rather than the function of their behavior. After each example, use the reflection prompts to identify the function of the narcissist's behavior and consider how the other person could respond differently by directly targeting this function rather than words and surface actions.

Lindsay and Grant

Lindsay was a sales rep for a prominent pharmaceutical company. Over the last year, she had not only reached her sales goals but surpassed them, and she was the best-performing sales rep within her division. Recently, her company had merged with another large pharmaceutical company, changing the managerial structure of several departments. Lindsay was informed that she had been selected out of hundreds of employees to interview for a new managerial position. The position also came with a considerable pay increase that would be life-changing for Lindsay, allowing her to finally be able to pay off her student debt.

Lindsay's interview was scheduled for 8:30 a.m. the next day with the vice president of sales and the head of human resources, both of whom Lindsay perceived as intimidating. She was simultaneously excited and nervous as she drove home from work, and she looked forward to sharing the good news with her husband, Grant.

She walked in the door, smiling ear to ear, and screamed out the good news to Grant. His response was less than enthusiastic. Instead of congratulating her, he berated her for forgetting to take the trash out that morning. "How can you possibly take on a new position when you can't even remember something that simple?"

Lindsay apologized for her forgetfulness, explaining that she had been running late that morning and forgot. Grant then continued to belittle her, reminding her of all the times she had forgotten to do things around the house and saying how she was extremely irresponsible . . . just like her own mother.

Lindsay started to cry. She began to defend her character, giving examples of how extremely responsible she was—and nothing like her mother. Grant and Lindsay argued back and forth for over an hour; Grant brought up numerous occasions that highlighted Lindsay's supposed lack of responsibility, and Lindsay offered detailed explanations as to why Grant was wrong. The fighting went on into the middle of the night, and with Lindsay's interview the next morning, she started to panic. Maybe she really *was* irresponsible. Maybe she wasn't qualified for the new position. The night was nothing like she had envisioned; if only she had just kept the good news to herself.

When Lindsay directly engaged in an argument with Grant, she became overwhelmed trying to justify her behavior, challenge his perception, and prove her worth. By responding to *what* Grant said (rather than *why*), Lindsay became entangled in doubt, confusion, and sadness, eventually leading her to question her own capabilities and identity.

Now, let's look at what would have happened if Lindsay had been able to identify and respond to the function of Grant's behavior rather than his words and actions.

Lindsay hurried home to inform Grant of her exciting news. She ran into the house, giving him a big hug and happily sharing her good news. Grant didn't congratulate her, but instead began to belittle her achievement, bringing to her attention several occasions in which he felt she had been forgetful and irresponsible. Not only had Lindsay forgotten to take out the trash that morning, but, Grant claimed, she had recently forgotten to close the garage door and neglected to pick up his medicine at the pharmacy. Grant told her she was selfish and questioned her ability to take on a new position when she couldn't even manage what was currently on her plate.

Although she was hurt by these accusations, Lindsay calmly walked into the kitchen, got a drink of water, and began to return emails on her phone. Grant followed her into the kitchen, explaining to her that he was just trying to protect her because he didn't want her to fail or get fired. Lindsay looked up from her phone, replied, "Thank you for your concern," and looked back down at her phone.

Grant continued to bring up times when Lindsay was overwhelmed and forgetful, to which she calmly stated, "Those were tough times, weren't they?" and continued returning emails. Grant insisted that Lindsay was setting herself up for failure, and he just wanted to help. Lindsay once again thanked him for his concern, which made Grant throw his hands up in the air and leave the room to go watch TV.

At first, Lindsay was understandably hurt by Grant's accusations, but over the years she learned that this behavior was a pattern. Whenever Lindsay demonstrated even the smallest act of independence and autonomy—a promotion, a night out with friends, lunch with her father, even buying clothes—Grant always provoked an unrelated argument. In the past, these arguments caused Lindsay such distress that she would cancel her plans to appease Grant and apologize for her "selfish and irresponsible" behavior. Now, however, she saw Grant's behavior for what it really was: manipulation and control. Rather than continue to engage in *what* Grant said and did, Lindsay found it to be more effective to respond to the *why*. In this case, the *why* is because Grant felt his grip on Lindsay slip anytime she expressed signs of independence. His arguing was nothinq more than a manipulative tactic to destabilize Lindsay's identity and regain control.

Rather than emotionally reacting to Grant's accusations and behavior, Lindsay responded to its function:

- She did not verbally respond to Grant.
- She left the room to go into the kitchen.
- She engaged in neutral behavior (got a drink of water) in the midst of Grant's screaming to appear unfazed and emotionally nonreactive. It is important to note that just because Lindsay appears composed,

it does *not* mean she isn't feeling uncomfortable emotions; it just means she is able to sit with those feelings *while* engaging in effective boundaries.

- She again engaged in behavior unrelated to the argument (checking emails).
- When questioned by Grant, her responses and body language remained neutral.

All of these behaviors share one goal: They target the function of Grant's behavior (i.e., gaining control) and deprive him of it.

What happened when Lindsay repeatedly defended herself against Grant's accusations in the first scenario?

____

____

____

____

Why is the outcome of the second scenario different?

____

____

____

____

Which scenario increases Lindsay's sense of control and empowerment? Why?

____

____

____

____

Norelle and Ivan

Norelle was heading to the airport to catch a flight to Florida for her best friend's bachelorette party. Her boyfriend, Ivan, knew that Norelle was going to be late for her flight. In fact, he'd purposely misplaced her passport just to increase her already heightened anxiety. Plus, he was annoyed because he wanted to watch the Eagles game at 2 p.m., and there was no way he would be back before halftime. When he asked her to just take a car service, Norelle was offended by his request and told him he was being inconsiderate. After arguing for a while, Ivan finally agreed to drive.

During the ride, Ivan continued to yell at Norelle, accusing her of being disrespectful of his time and only caring about herself and her friends. Norelle denied these accusations, giving Ivan repeated examples of all the times she had been overly respectful of Ivan and his needs. As soon as they approached the highway, Ivan sped up to around 100 miles per hour, weaving violently between lanes while Norelle pleaded with him to slow down. Ivan shot back, "Well, maybe if you had been more organized in the first place, I wouldn't have to drive so fast."

By the time they arrived at the airport, Norelle was in tears. She apologized to Ivan for the argument, but he ignored her, dropped her bags off on the curb, and drove off.

What behavioral patterns and manipulative tactics do you see in this scenario?

____

____

____

____

What could this scenario look like if Norelle responded to the function of Ivan's behavior rather than his words and actions?

____

____

____

____

Dante and Claire

After fifteen years of marriage, Dante was leaving Claire. Multiple false promises of change and a complete lack of accountability had pushed Dante to his limit—he finally had enough. It was having an impact on his physical health, his mental well-being, and even his career. Dante had made several attempts to leave over the years, but Claire's false promises of change and her threats to take the children away had always sucked him back into the relationship. The couple had been through years of marriage therapy, with multiple therapists, but Claire would never continue treatment, claiming that the therapist "always sided with Dante."

However, years of infidelity and psychological and emotional abuse had finally taken their toll on Dante. He contacted a family attorney and found an apartment near the family home so that he could continue to see his two children.

One day, when Dante was picking up the children for the weekend, Claire asked him yet again if he would go to couples therapy to attempt reconciliation, to which Dante calmly and appropriately declined. Claire continued to pressure Dante into therapy, telling him that a "good father" would try to make his marriage work. She continued to push his buttons, calling him a terrible father who consistently neglected his children to satisfy his own needs. Dante spent the next 30 minutes explaining to Claire, yet again, how all their attempts to reconcile had failed and he needed to move on for his own well-being.

When Dante returned after the weekend to drop off the children, Claire immediately began berating Dante's decision to go forward with the divorce. Finally, Dante could no longer remain quiet. He screamed back at Claire in front of the children—something he'd sworn he'd never do. Claire simply laughed in response. As she ushered the children into the house, she said loudly, "And you say *I'm* the one who needs help?"

What behavioral patterns and manipulative tactics do you see in this scenario?

____

____

____

____

What could this scenario look like if Dante responded to the function of Claire's behavior rather than her words?

____

____

____

____

Harry and Carol

Harry had recently been offered a new position in his company that would require him to move across the country from California to New York City. It was a promotion with a significant pay increase that carried with it significant opportunity for growth. He was single, had no children, and figured now was a perfect opportunity to take this leap. Harry's family, friends, and colleagues were thrilled for him, except for his mother, Carol. Carol did not think Harry was making a good decision, despite all the obvious benefits this career change offered. Interestingly, Carol could never come up with a concrete reason Harry should turn down the offer, except to say that he knew no one in NYC. She couldn't understand why Harry would be so excited to leave his family and move 3,000 miles away. "Am I that bad of a mother?" she asked. Harry did feel guilty moving away, but he was 26, and it was time.

Shortly after Harry signed the commitment letter with his company, he began noticing that some of his family members, specifically his two aunts, had stopped reaching out to him. They weren't returning his emails or texts, and they had unfollowed him on social media. Confused, he called his mother. According to Carol, they were furious with him for suddenly leaving with little concern for his mother's feelings.

One day, Harry received a text message from a longtime family friend, urging Harry to seek treatment for his depression and saying his entire extended family and close family friends were very worried about his impulsive decision to transport himself across the country on a whim. Unbeknownst to Harry, his mother had been telling relatives and friends that his move was the result of hasty and immature decision-making, likely to be the result of long-standing mental health problems. She also claimed that Harry "probably was moving there for some girl."

Harry was furious. He contacted his family members and tried his best to combat the rumors. He even sent an email to Carol to reassure her that he would never abandon her and that he loves her very much, but in the end, he only ended up more angry and emotionally exhausted.

What behavioral patterns and manipulative tactics do you see in this scenario?

___

___

___

___

What could this scenario look like if Harry responded to the function of his mother's behavior rather than her words?

Take a minute to think about a time when you responded directly to a narcissist's words and surface actions rather than their function. Describe the details of the interaction.

- Where were you?
- Who were you with?
- What occurred?
- What was said? (Include your responses.)
- How did you feel in the moment?
- What was the outcome of the interaction?

If you had responded to the behavior's *function*, what would the interaction have looked/sounded like?

____

____

____

____

Would this approach have resulted in a different outcome? Explain.

____

____

____

____

ACT Concept

Gain Objectivity

I tell every single client at the onset of therapy that, eventually, they will hit a point where everything clicks—when they can see the predictable pattern of the narcissist's behaviors. This is because once you can identify the narcissist's playbook, you gain *objectivity* to their patterns of coercive control. In other words, you begin seeing the narcissist's behaviors as separate from yourself, rather than as your responsibility or a reflection of your worth.

ACT and mindfulness-based strategies are essential for reaching this point—they help you step back, observe without judgment, and clearly identify the patterns that once kept you emotionally and psychologically entangled. It becomes almost like watching a play you've seen several times before; often, you'll find you already know their next line before they deliver it.

Once you gain this objectivity, your confusion and self-doubt will slowly begin to shift toward clarity, and your trust in your perception of reality will gradually be restored. You'll feel more in control of your own emotional responses and learn to maintain effective boundaries targeted specifically toward the underlying function of the narcissist's behaviors.

The three steps described in this chapter (recognizing tactics, observing context, and identifying function) don't just reveal the narcissist's abuse patterns; they offer you the benefit of predictability within the chaos. Just as social scripts of everyday life guide you in how to respond in situations, recognizing the narcissist's script offers you some sense of direction and control. Your ability to identify the patterns of abuse allows you to predict how and when the behaviors will show up and, more importantly, how to engage in effective boundaries.

4

Boundaries

Imagine that you clean out your nightstand and find, in the very back of the drawer, a bunch of necklaces that are completely knotted together. You pick up the twisted mess of chains and try to untangle them, but in doing so, you make the knots worse. You spend the next forty minutes unsuccessfully trying to untangle your necklaces, but the more you engage with the knotted mess, the worse it becomes. Looking up, you realize that the time you've spent working on the necklaces has made you late for a Zoom meeting with your boss. Not only are you angry about your jewelry, but now you are anxious about being late for your meeting.

What's the most helpful thing you could do in this situation? Clearly, it would be to stop trying to fix the jewelry and simply put it down. Will it still be a tangled mess? Yes. But will it continue to consume your energy and time? No. By putting the jewelry aside, even though it remains knotted, you're accomplishing two things: First, it eliminates the possibility of the situation getting worse by continuing to engage without the proper tools, and second, it frees you to invest your time and energy into the things you value, like being a reliable employee.

The tangled necklace mirrors what happens with those in narcissistic abusive relationships. The more you wrestle with self-doubt, blame, guilt, justification of the abuse, the urge to make sense of their contradictions, and your need to prove your worth, the more you become entangled in the narcissist's narrative. Just like the jewelry, your attention and emotions become fixated on the chaos, consuming your time, energy, and emotional resources while pulling you further away from your own self-identity and values.

But of course, narcissistic abuse is not as simple as tangled jewelry, and it's unlikely the narcissist in your life is going to remain neatly in the drawer, as it were. So, now that we have that distance in place, the question becomes: what do we do next?

The answer is boundaries.

Boundaries—A Narcissist's Worst Enemy

Boundaries are our way of letting people know what behavior we are willing, and not willing, to accept; they inform people of how we wish to be treated. Recall that most of our long-standing behavioral patterns form in childhood. In the same way, boundaries are influenced by what we perceive as safe and acceptable from our early caregivers and environment. These experiences teach us to protect our needs, respond to others, and essentially come to understand where we end and someone else begins. If someone leans away from us or stiffens up in response to a hug, they would probably like more personal space, or if they become vague or noncommittal in a conversation, they may be uncomfortable with the topic, and so we adjust our behavior accordingly by changing the topic or apologizing. We make these adjustments out of respect for others' boundaries because we don't want to cause them discomfort, and because we too want our boundaries respected.

When people struggle to read social cures, it can sometimes seem like they are disregarding our boundaries. In reality, it is not always a deliberate attempt to ignore or disrespect us; it is simply that they don't notice or recognize the signals we are giving. By clearly communicating and modeling our boundaries, we make it easier for them to become aware and respond appropriately. It's an unspoken social contract—to be in a healthy relationship of any kind, or even to have a brief interaction with the cashier at the market, we need to recognize the other person's boundaries, honor our own, and respond in ways that make room for both.

But keep in mind, not everyone grows up in an environment where boundaries are clearly modeled and reinforced. In abusive, neglectful, or unpredictable homes, these early experiences can lead to significant confusion about what is considered appropriate and can result in blurred and inconsistent boundaries as we grow and interact with others. While these formative circumstances in childhood shape adult behavior and impact our relationships, most people not only develop awareness of how their behavior affects others, but they also care enough to change it, even when it may be scary.

In contrast, a narcissist isn't someone who struggles to notice or understand boundaries. Rather, they are attracted to boundaries precisely because they want to override them. They seek control and power by deliberately disregarding and manipulating people's boundaries. They show little empathy for the damage and hurt they inflict and have no intention of adjusting their behaviors (unless it benefits them directly). This is why the early stages of a narcissistic relationship are marked by such disarming flattery, interest, and intimacy to create the illusion of connection—the narcissist draws you into a false sense of trust and safety, subtly manipulating you into lowering your guard.

Because this occurs incrementally over time, you may initially misinterpret the narcissist's increasing boundary violations, particularly during the love-bombing stage, as a reflection of deep connection and love. During the relationship, the narcissist's views, opinions, and perceptions of you become so entangled with your internal dialogue and self-identity, you are no longer able to differentiate their voice from your own. This subtle and intermittent psychological conditioning allows the narcissist's boundary violations to go on unnoticed long after the idealization stage has ended. The narcissist wants to blur, and eventually eradicate, the space between your voice and theirs so that eventually, you are no longer able to recognize where your self-identity ends and theirs begins.

Gaining awareness and ownership of your boundaries helps you disrupt the narcissist's intrusion and influence over your internal world. Through recovering, rebuilding, and maintaining healthy boundaries, you can begin to reclaim the mental space necessary to rebuild your core self.

A Better Understanding of Boundaries

It can be extremely uncomfortable, even scary, to set a boundary, especially for someone who has had difficulty setting boundaries for most of their life. People avoid setting boundaries for various reasons: they are fearful, confused, trying to avoid conflict and keep the peace, or hoping to minimize the risk of further abuse and punishment. Some people struggle to set boundaries, not because they don't want to, but because they never learned to recognize when a boundary would protect or benefit them. Someone who grew up believing they must be perfect to be valued may never say no to extra work, favors, or emotional demands in adulthood. Because they've been conditioned to see their needs as "less than," they may not even see a boundary as necessary. A child who is taught that expressing anger is wrong may never assert themself when someone crosses a line in their adult relationships.

This is why narcissistic abusers often employ intimidation as a manipulative tactic to discourage people from asserting themselves so that they are easier to control. Over time, you grow to doubt the value of your boundaries and are fearful that setting a boundary will lead to increased punishment and abuse. It is important to recognize that your perceived inability to establish boundaries within a narcissistic abusive relationship does *not* reflect an inherent weakness; there is nothing wrong with you. You are simply trying to survive. You have been deliberately conditioned and manipulated into remaining silent, undervaluing yourself, and diminishing your self-worth. This is not your fault; it is the result of the narcissist's calculated actions.

With any uncomfortable behavior, if you wait until you feel completely at ease before you act, you may never begin. The same applies to setting boundaries. If you wait until you "feel ready" or until the situation improves to your standards, you will only prolong the very emotional discomfort you're trying to avoid by not setting the boundary in the first place. Waiting to feel ready keeps you stuck while increasing the discomfort.

ACT Concept

Move Forward Through Discomfort

Many approaches to therapy focus on resolving negative feelings and challenging or changing thoughts to pave the way for behavior change. But being in a relationship with a narcissist makes this a moving target—they will always find ways to undercut your growth and sabotage your efforts to change. Waiting to act on your own behalf until you feel worthy and confident means staying where you are, mired in the narcissist's vicious cycle. It deprives you of creating a new experience that proves to yourself you *can* do this despite the overwhelming discomfort you may have.

Imagine you're scheduled to speak in front of a crowd of 300 people—and you hate speaking in public. If you waited until you felt ready, you'd likely be waiting a long time. While delaying may reduce your anxiety in the moment, the relief is short-lived. By avoiding your discomfort, you convince your brain that these feelings are dangerous, ultimately ensuring your anxiety will be even worse next time. It also confirms your belief that you are incapable of not only public speaking, but also managing painful emotions. However, if you step up on stage and give the presentation *while* feeling anxious, your discomfort will gradually diminish as you proceed. Not only does this kind of experience teach you that it's possible to move through discomfort and anxiety, but it also gives you hard evidence of your capability that you can draw upon when faced with difficult tasks or uncomfortable feelings in the future.

ACT can support you in reclaiming your identity outside of the narcissist's control by guiding you to take action *despite* the bad feelings you may have. It teaches you how to feel the fear, shame, and anxiety while at the same time acting in ways that align you with what you value.

To help you persist despite the discomfort, it's important to understand in detail what purpose boundaries serve and how exactly they can change the dynamic of your relationship. This is where a lot of online content goes awry, leading to incorrect assumptions and misconceptions about boundaries.

Assumptions About Boundaries

The goal of boundaries in a healthy relationship is to ensure that both people feel safe, autonomous, and confident about trusting each other. The narcissist, however, views your boundary as a threat to their control, and they will attack it to undermine your autonomy and strip away your sense of self. Without understanding the behavioral nuances of this personality structure, people often rely on ineffective strategies that inadvertently lead to a deeper entanglement in these harmful dynamics. You might assume that you can take the same approach you would with a non-narcissistic person. Not only is this ineffective, but it can escalate the abuse and leave you feeling even more confused and hopeless.

When establishing boundaries within a narcissistic dynamic, you must understand *how, why,* and *when* a boundary should be used. Boundaries with a narcissistic *must* be carefully tailored to the function of the narcissist's behavior, not their actions and words. These boundaries are for your benefit alone; a narcissist will rarely accept them willingly. The ultimate goal is to create boundaries that allow you to walk away with a sense of neutrality, empowerment, and peace. It is this neutrality that strips the narcissist of their control over you.

Imagine that you are invited to your friend's birthday dinner. While you are getting ready for the evening, your partner tells you they are concerned about how much money you will be spending at the dinner. They accuse you of being irresponsible, having no concept of money, and being the sole reason for all their financial difficulties.

In a healthy relationship, this discussion might also come up, whether it's because your partner feels you've made mistakes in the past around spending or simply because they've always been overly cautious with their finances. But it could be resolved by honest, respectful acknowledgment of their concerns while also asserting your wants and needs. You might say, "I hear what you're saying, and I want you to feel comfortable. I don't want to cancel on my friend when it's her birthday, but would you feel okay if I limit my spending to a certain amount tonight? We can definitely keep talking about this issue—it's important to me that we are on the same page about money." Neither partner's goal is to gain control over the other, gaslight, or diminish the other's sense of agency. And while these words don't resolve the issue once and for all, it is a productive conversation that maintains your autonomy both financially and socially.

If you said those same words to a narcissistic partner, it is likely they would have zero intention to find a mutual solution and would use your response as fuel to escalate an argument. This is because their point in raising this issue has nothing to do with your fiscal responsibility; it is to ruin your evening, further convince you that you are inferior, and ultimately, gain control over your emotions and behavior. They might answer you with escalation (e.g., "Don't talk down to me!"), aggrieved blame ("Typical of you to choose your friends over me"), or a cold shoulder ("Fine, do whatever you want") followed by leaving the room and slamming the door. Whether their response persuades you to cancel your plans, undermines your self-confidence, or ensures that you are unable to enjoy your night out, they'll have accomplished their goal.

Three Misconceptions of Boundaries

Misconception #1: By setting a boundary, you can control someone's behavior toward you.

The goal of a boundary is not to change someone else's behavior or make them act the way you want. For example, you can tell your friend that if they continue to be late and disregard your schedule, you will unfortunately need to stop making plans with them. But you can't make them show up on time.

Boundaries are best understood as a user manual—not for you, but for people who want to interact with you. How people ultimately decide to respond to your boundaries—whether they follow your user manual or not—is out of your control. You only have control of your own responses and behaviors, and the degree to which you're able to regulate your thoughts and emotions in a given situation. The goal of a boundary is to help you remain grounded in your values and self-worth, regardless of how another person acts.

Misconception #2: If someone chooses not to respect your boundary, it means your boundary didn't work.

I have helped countless clients develop healthy boundaries, only for them to come back the next session and tell me their boundaries failed. The reason was always the same: "I tried to set my boundary, but they didn't listen."

For example, imagine someone repeatedly interrupts you during conversations. Of course, this frustrates you, maybe even angers you, but rather than showing frustration or engaging in an argument, you acknowledge your emotions and, at the same time, calmly say, "I would like to finish my thought." Then you continue speaking. This neutral, steady response constitutes a successful boundary for you, even if they continue to interrupt.

The effectiveness of your boundary isn't determined by whether others follow or disregard it. The only measure of success is whether it helps you remain connected to what matters to you, independent of the other person's response. This is especially true within the context of a narcissistic abusive relationship.

Misconception #3: If you still experience difficult feelings despite holding your boundary, the boundary didn't work.

Holding strong on your boundaries doesn't always mean feeling strong while you do it. On the outside, you may look calm and in control of your emotions, while on the inside you're screaming in frustration or sobbing with grief. That is completely okay. Experiencing these very appropriate emotions does not mean your boundary failed; it means you are human, and humans long to connect with each other. However, with repeated practice in maintaining your boundary, this new behavior will eventually match how you feel inside.

Two Types of Boundaries

There are two types of boundaries you can set within a narcissistic relationship: external and internal. *External* (behavioral) boundaries are those that are directly observable by the narcissist and others, while *internal* (emotional and cognitive) boundaries are those that are experienced directly by the owner of the boundary. The type of boundary you choose to set depends on multiple factors, such as the frequency of the behavior, the type of behavior, whether this boundary has been set in the past, and of course, the context of the situation.

Boundary Types

External Boundaries	Internal Boundaries
Body posture	Mood states
Eye contact	Thought process
Words spoken	Self-talk
Tone of voice	Expectations of self and others
Mannerisms	Self-narrative
Observable actions taken	

External Boundaries

You're probably most familiar with the concept of external boundaries. These include any behaviors that are directly observable, such as body language, eye contact, tone of voice, word choice, facial expression, and actions. You may express a boundary by not answering a work call on the weekend, saying no to hosting a holiday dinner because you're too overwhelmed with work, or choosing not to engage in family arguments by stepping away or changing the subject. In a narcissistic relationship, you might block the individual's email and social media accounts, limit the time you spend with them, or withhold personal details in a conversation. External boundaries are extremely important, but they are only as effective as your ability to maintain them.

Internal Boundaries

Internal boundaries are the emotional and cognitive guidelines you set for yourself to protect the integrity of your thoughts, feelings, and sense of who you are. They shape how you respond to what's happening inside you. As these boundaries grow stronger, it becomes easier to pause and choose how to act instead of reacting purely on emotion.

If you are subjected to prolonged narcissistic abuse, you will likely come to believe that your internal boundaries are wrong, ineffective, and cannot be trusted. This can make setting and maintaining internal boundaries difficult. As confusing and frightening as it is to have your boundaries stripped down over time by the narcissist, it can be equally confusing and frightening to begin rebuilding them. To begin rebuilding, you must redefine what you're willing to tolerate and then hold these boundaries in the face of ongoing manipulation, fear, and self-doubt. It's understandable that maintaining internal boundaries feels incredibly difficult. To increase the likelihood of consistently maintaining your boundaries even while experiencing uncomfortable feelings and thoughts, it is important to learn how to regulate your emotions.

Emotional Regulation

In addition to gaining awareness of your internal world, learning to regulate emotions is a key component of ACT that proves essential for setting internal boundaries. When emotions are unregulated (e.g., avoided, suppressed), they can infiltrate your thoughts and influence your behaviors in ways that are unhealthy, allowing them to override your values-driven behavior. For example, if you are incredibly anxious in face-to-face interactions, you might avoid an in-person interview even though it may be exactly the type of job for which you've been searching.

Regulating emotions doesn't mean eliminating them or even trying to reduce them; it means creating enough internal space to simply tolerate the emotions. Think of your emotions and all that is part of your internal world as if they are passengers in a car. The riders are loud, chaotic, and rude—but they don't get to take control of the steering wheel. They can ride in the car next to you *without* being allowed to drive. Are the annoying passengers still in the car? Yes. Are they irritating? Yes. Are you still able to drive the car? Yes. Even with the noise? Yes. Regulating your emotions will make it increasingly easier to maintain your boundaries (e.g., refusing to take on more work because you're at your limit) even when intense emotions and thoughts are present (e.g., "If I say no to working, I'm lazy").

ACT Concept

Separate Yourself from the Abuse Cycle

One of the principles of ACT is accepting that your thoughts and emotions occur *separately* from you. In the case of narcissistic abuse, you can learn to perceive coercive control and manipulation as occurring outside of you. This creates space for you to identify the narcissist's specific behavior patterns and gain the clarity to form effective boundaries. From this distance, you can see their hurtful words and manipulative behaviors for what they really are—tools for control, not reflections of your own personal worth.

Stepping outside your internal struggle and viewing it as an observer can give you an overwhelming sense of freedom and empowerment. All the energy you've spent trying to *not* feel the bad feelings and *not* think the negative thoughts can now be redirected toward the people, interests, and goals you value most in life, helping you move forward on your path to reclaiming your sense of self.

Let's say you establish a boundary for yourself that you are no longer responding to your narcissistic ex's ranting texts. Then they message you, begging for forgiveness and sending screenshots of two first-class tickets to France. Immediately, a rush of guilt, panic, and fear overwhelm you. "I am a terrible person," "I hated when my ex ignored my best efforts, and now I'm doing that to them." "Maybe *I'm* the narcissist!" You suddenly feel overwhelmed and confused. Through years of manipulation and gaslighting, the narcissist has crushed any confidence you had left in your ability to trust your own judgment. You've always had to rely on them to define and validate your internal experiences.

To best regulate your emotions, you must first create the distance, or internal space, we spoke about previously. Notice your thoughts and feelings as they come up; observe your thoughts as words that are written on a wall rather than inside your mind. Don't put any effort into trying to avoid, get rid of, or challenge anything that comes up. Simply be an observer of *you*. Notice your feelings and thoughts in response to your decision to not text your ex back: "I feel guilt and sadness." "What if I'm being too petty? It *is* Paris. That is not cheap." Don't analyze, defend, or justify—just observe.

How to Handle Anxiety

You'll notice that anxiety will often surge when you are trying to create or enforce a boundary—especially if you are new at setting them. There are many exercises you can try to regulate the nervous system when feelings arise. Breathing exercises are a great place to start. See chapter 6 and the Fishbowl Breathing exercise (see page 209) as you notice the thoughts and feelings of anxiety move through your body.

Remember, the goal is not to get rid of your anxiety; it is to untangle you from chaos and create space to feel your feelings without acting on them in a way that would be inconsistent with your values. In our example, you want to ignore the text message and sit with your emotions rather than immediately grabbing your phone and feverishly texting back because it feels too unbearable not to respond.

As you observe your thoughts and feel your feelings, remember to consider the *function* of the narcissist's behavior—what do you recognize is happening? In this example, we can see that your ex is *hoovering*. Knowing that the narcissist is using a specific control tactic, you can look *at* your uncomfortable emotions as a manufactured product of their manipulation. They *want* you to feel this way. Standing in the space you created, you can see the text for what it is—a test to break your boundaries and allow them to regain access to your internal world. By becoming an observer of your emotions and thoughts, rather than getting tangled up within them or trying to get rid of them by texting back, you remain committed to your boundaries rather than being pulled back into your ex's chaos.

Eventually, as you build confidence and reclaim your power, maintaining your internal boundaries will no longer feel as frightening but instead will become a vital and reliable source of self-validation. Boundaries will start being a daily reminder that you're entitled to feel however you want, particularly in response to the actions of someone committed to misunderstanding and hurting you. Be assured that you don't have to have all this in place before you can begin disentangling yourself from the narcissistic dynamic. Each small step forward helps you grow in strength and self-worth, proving to yourself that you are fully capable of reclaiming your power and acting in the best interest of your values.

REFLECTION

Now that you've learned about both external and internal boundaries, use the following story and reflection questions to understand how both come into play when you're entangled within the cycle of narcissistic abuse.

Debbie and Milly

Debbie was dreading Christmas dinner at her in-laws' house. Every year it was the same: Debbie's mother-in-law Milly would begin asking about Debbie's fertility issues, commenting about her weight, and questioning her career choice. Milly would make passive-aggressive comments throughout the tension-filled evening, and an argument would inevitably erupt between Debbie and her husband, Gary, on the drive home. Debbie would accuse Gary of not being supportive, while he felt that she was being overly sensitive and that his mother was only "trying to be helpful because she cares."

This year, Debbie decided she was no longer going to tolerate Milly's digs; this time she was going to set very strict boundaries. She chose to drive separately from Gary, allowing her the freedom to leave whenever she decided. She also had a set time she planned to leave. If approached with questions about her fertility, body image, or career, she would respond with "I'm not comfortable discussing that now" in a calm, monotone voice, repeating this mantra as many times as needed reqardless of her mother-in-law's responses. She also planned to excuse herself to use the bathroom, get a drink, or take a phone call if the conversation took an uncomfortable turn.

As expected, at Christmas dinner, Milly began pushing Debbie to discuss her latest fertility treatment, asking her if the doctor had any fast-acting solutions to her weight gain from the hormone injections. Rather than respond out of anger and frustration, such as a passive-aggressive comment or an obvious eye roll, Debbie looked her mother-in-law in the eyes, smiled, and calmy stated, "I'm not comfortable discussing this right now." Then she politely excused herself to carry some empty dinner plates to the sink.

Milly offered to help carry the dishes to the kitchen, following behind her and continuing to ask about Debbie's fertility. Again, Debbie calmly responded with her same mantra and continued washing dishes. When Milly saw she was not getting the heightened emotional response she wanted from Debbie, she shifted the conversation to Debbie's decision to take a promotion at work. Milly expressed concern that Gary may feel neglected if Debbie started spending more time at the office. In the past, this comment would have sent Debbie into a tailspin. But this time, she acknowledged her internal emotions and, rather than act on them, she did not respond. Instead, she stated that it was getting late and she needed to get to bed, as she had to wake up early the next morning. She thanked Milly for dinner, kissed Gary goodbye, told him she loved him and would see him at home, and left.

If we use Milly's response as a barometer to measure the success of Debbie's boundaries, it appears as if they failed. In no way did they stop Milly from making passive-aggressive comments. But if we measure the success of Debbie's boundaries by the degree to which Debbie was able to regulate her emotions and walk away from the situation feeling more empowered, we can conclude that her boundaries were effective. Had she engaged in familiar response patterns to avoid her internal discomfort, such as yelling at Milly, it is likely she would have ended up feeling even more of the frustration and lack of control that she was trying to get rid of. Instead, Debbie's willingness to sit with those feelings in the moment and still maintain her boundaries resulted in a sense of empowerment and control.

Think of a time when you did not set a boundary because it was too uncomfortable. Record the details using the following prompts:

Where were you?

Who were you with at the time?

Describe the details of the interaction.

___

___

___

Why did you not set a boundary?

___

___

___

What boundaries do you wish you had set?

___

___

___

Are these boundaries internal, external, or both?

___

___

Would these boundaries have changed your experience of the situation? Explain.

___

___

___

A Healthy Basis for Boundaries

Remember, the true purpose of a boundary is to help you walk away from an interaction feeling more empowered, but the way you set boundaries with a narcissist will look different and may shift depending on the situation. Simply drawing a line in the sand won't be nearly as effective; they'll be only too eager to walk right over it. To ensure your boundary is most effective in protecting your peace and agency, it's important to form your boundary on a basis that is strategic to the situation while remaining authentic to your values.

Boundaries Based on a Specific Function

We know that within the context of a narcissistic abusive relationship, determining the underlying function of the narcissist's behavior is essential. This function must be the cornerstone that shapes every response you give, every boundary you set, and every move you make with a narcissist. In fact, the words and superficial details of your interaction with them matter very little. What truly matters is what lies beneath their behaviors, threats, and words—and that is always their need for power, dominance, and control over you. The *why* reveals their underlying intent, and it is this awareness that informs your boundaries.

For example, perhaps your narcissistic spouse starts an argument with you on the night of your son's college graduation. The subject of the argument? You forgot to buy eggs yesterday. As you listen to them criticize your thoughtlessness and lack of responsibility, a functional approach would have you ask yourself "Why are they choosing to argue about this particular topic at this specific time?" rather than getting sucked into defending yourself for not purchasing the eggs. The answer to the *why* in this case is that they wanted to gain access to and control of your emotions on a day that is very meaningful for you—a day where your focus isn't on your spouse, but on someone else's achievements. The forgetting of the eggs was deliberately chosen because your spouse knows that one of your deepest insecurities is the fear of being a neglectful parent who is dismissive of their family's needs. Your spouse's primary goal was to use your deepest vulnerabilities against you to create chaos, redirect attention onto themself, and manipulate your feelings.

Fortunately, your awareness of their true intent is what guides your response. You calmly say, "Yep, I forgot the eggs, but right now I am focused on our son's graduation." Instead of getting caught up in the details of forgetting the eggs and the need to defend your responsible nature, this statement cuts straight to your spouse's manipulative efforts. It also challenges their attempt to assert dominance over a situation where they are not the focus.

The clarity gained by recognizing the function behind the narcissist's coercively controlling behaviors, rather than getting lost in the words and surface details, prepares you to anticipate these dynamics, such as during occasions where your spouse isn't the center of your attention. It helps you to separate yourself from their manipulation and form effective responses that target their true intent, rather than becoming entangled within their chaos.

REFLECTION

Using the previous scenario of your son's graduation, what would be another example of a function-based boundary?

____

____

____

For this same scenario, what is an example of a boundary that is not function-based?

___

___

___

Of these two example boundaries, which would you find more uncomfortable to set and maintain? Why?

___

___

___

Would these two boundaries produce different outcomes? If so, what are the potential outcomes?

___

___

___

Which boundary would produce the healthiest outcome for you? Why?

___

___

___

Boundaries Based on Values

We know that engaging in behaviors that align with your values leads to a more fulfilled life, while behaviors that take you further away from your values can put you at risk for increased stress, dissatisfaction in relationships, mental health difficulties, and even physical health issues over time. This not only reinforces the importance of identifying your core values, but it also highlights the need to be mindful of whether your daily actions are moving you toward those values or pulling you away from them.

ACT Concept

Ground Yourself in Your Values

Values work is a key feature of ACT and an integral part of healing from narcissistic abuse. It starts with asking the fundamental question: "What are your core values?" Not what someone else told you they should be, or what you believed them to be as a necessary means for survival, but what truly matters to you. ACT holds space for you to uncover, reshape, and reformulate your own set of independent values that do not include the influence of the narcissist and their narrative.

Your values become anchor points, offering stability, a sense of control, and self-guidance when you're deciding what boundaries to set, what relationships to entertain, what parenting decisions to make, and even what clothes you buy and what music to listen to.

Values stabilize your behavior, particularly during times of heightened stress and emotional chaos. No matter what emotions arise, acting in service of your values keeps you moving forward in the right direction. Simply put, if you have always based your boundaries on a particular feeling (e.g., "I need to feel calm to set my boundary"), your ability to maintain that boundary will collapse. Moods are moving targets, whereas values are anchor points. Behaving in ways that align with your values while sitting with your emotions (e.g., guilt, fear, shame) makes it more likely you will be successful in setting and maintaining your boundary. Your behavior no longer requires emotional permission.

When we remain rooted in our values, our actions become far more effective against the narcissist's manipulation and coercive control because they are no longer reactive. Values-driven actions are not based on fluctuating emotions, but rather on your own self-direction. Ask yourself: Am I acting in accordance with my values, yes or no? As a result of acting in line with your values, common coercive control tactics—such as gaslighting, instilling guilt, hoovering, and other forms of psychological abuse—lose their effectiveness and leverage. When anchored in values, your actions are no longer at the mercy of your emotional state. Even if the narcissist increases their efforts to distort your reality or blame you for their problems, you can remain oriented toward what you value most rather than focusing on the narcissist's emotions. Most importantly, it debunks the misconception that being strong, confident, or calm are prerequisites for you to establish boundaried responses.

REFLECTION

Elisa and Gayle

Elisa took a new job at the same company as Gayle, and the two became fast friends, appearing to have several things in common. Both were newly divorced, both had recently moved to Philadelphia, and both had expressed their commitment to establishing their career. What began as shared lunch breaks quickly turned into after-work dinners and weekend plans. A few months into their friendship, they decided to move in together to save money, but also because of the emotional comfort living together offered.

At first, everything ran smoothly. They split all expenses, commuted to work together, and helped one another unwind after a stressful workday. But about three months in, Elisa started noticing some changes in Gayle's behavior. For example, Gayle started questioning Elisa about eating food that "wasn't hers," despite their joint food shopping. At first, Elisa brushed it off as stress or a simple miscommunication. But the comments didn't stop; in fact, they became constant and more hurtful. Over time, Gayle grew increasingly more critical about household rules. She yelled at Elisa for incorrectly loading the dishwasher and doing a poor job cleaning the common area, even though Gayle refused to take on any chores. When Elisa invited a friend over, Gayle insisted she must first ask for permission. When Elisa made plans that didn't include Gayle, she was told she was a selfish friend and a lousy roommate. When Elisa's family came to visit, Gayle became so enraged that she packed a bag and left for days without contacting Elisa to share where she was.

Elisa began walking on eggshells. She monitored her tone, her words, and her behavior just to avoid setting Gayle off. She found herself constantly distracted, exhausted, and less present, which began to take a toll on her productivity at work—something that Elisa took great pride in. Due to the stress and anxiety of living with Gayle, Elisa was missing deadlines, doubting her abilities and intelligence, and feeling physically exhausted from the many late nights spent defending herself against Gayle's accusations.

After receiving a not-so-generous performance evaluation by her boss, Elisa had finally had enough. Instead of wasting energy avoiding conflict and catering to Gayle's unpredictable nature, she started setting boundaries for herself. Rather than asking herself "What can I do so that Gayle doesn't get angry with me?" she began to ask herself a different question: "How is my behavior, and this relationship, enhancing my life?" and more specifically, "How are my efforts to maintain peace with Gayle impacting my ability to fully show up in my career?"

A week later, Elisa was invited to a prestigious sales training in Ohio. It was an opportunity she couldn't pass up, especially after her latest performance evaluation. Two days into the training, she received a text message from Gayle that said "I don't feel well. This is an emergency. I think I need to go to the hospital, and I don't trust anyone else to take me." Gayle was well aware of Elisa's need to always take care of others before herself, and this was her attempt to exploit it. This time, however, Elisa didn't avoid her guilt by giving in to Gayle's manipulation. Instead, she identified Gayle's underlying intent by asking herself "Why is she texting me this specific message at this specific time?" Elisa knew it wasn't a coincidence that Gayle texted her during this sales training; she had made it very clear throughout their relationship just how much she valued not only her career but also being a dependable and productive employee. Elisa saw Gayle's text not for what it *said*, but for what it *was*: an attempt to cause chaos during an important moment in her career, ruin the experience by instilling guilt, and gain power over Elisa's thoughts, emotions, and behaviors.

Even though Elisa still felt intense anxiety and guilt, she didn't allow it to dictate her next move. In the past, this may have looked like leaving the meeting to jump on the next flight home, apologizing profusely for not being there for Gayle, or texting back and forth all day, at the expense of her training, to defend Gayle's accusations that she only cared about her career and was a selfish friend—all of which are behaviors that are in direct opposition to Elisa's values. Elisa acknowledged her anxiety as it came over her, but this time, she responded to Gayle in a way that aligned with her value of showing up fully and professionally in her career. She did not leave the meeting, she did not engage in repetitive texting, and she did not apologize. Instead, she waited until the group had a breakout session, and in a calm, neutral tone (while still feeling scared internally), she sent the following text to Gayle: "I'm in my sales meeting in Ohio. If this is a true emergency and you don't want to contact another friend, you need to call 911 or go to the emergency room." She then silenced her phone and refocused her attention back to the meeting.

It is important to point out that sending this message didn't necessarily make Elisa less anxious. In fact, because it was a new behavior for Elisa, it may have even made her *more* nervous. Nor did Elisa's boundary prevent Gayle from sending her tons of angry texts over the next few days. However, as explained earlier, setting a values-consistent boundary isn't about changing the narcissist's behaviors or moods; it is about *you* engaging in behaviors that take you closer to what matters most to you, something that is critical when navigating and healing from narcissistic abuse.

After reading this scenario, what can you identify as something you personally value?

____

____

____

Describe a time when the narcissist in your life manipulated you into making behavioral choices that took you away from your values. Were your responses beneficial? Did your actions at the time make you feel better or worse in the moment?

____

____

____

Looking back now, what would you say was the true intention of their efforts?

____

____

____

What is an example of a values-driven boundary that could have been more effective in your situation? What do you anticipate the outcome would have been in the moment? How might you have felt?

____

____

____

Knowing what you now understand about the role of values-based boundaries, how might a values-guided approach in your interactions with the narcissist have changed not only the relationship itself, but also the relationship you have with yourself over time?

____

____

____

Unhealthy Basis for Boundaries

You've seen how establishing boundaries that are both function-based and values-driven can help you see through the deliberate manipulation and chaos created by the narcissist and move forward with empowerment and purpose. It's worthwhile to be aware of the kinds of boundaries that are *not* effective.

Boundaries Based on Emotional Avoidance

When a boundary is set primarily to avoid feeling bad in the moment, whether that feeling is anxiety, shame, selfishness, or guilt, it is unlikely that the boundary will be aligned with your values. Although this type of behavior may temporarily reduce your emotional or cognitive pain, it carries a significant long-term cost. Boundaries rooted in avoidance teach you not only that bad thoughts and feelings are intolerable, but also that you are incapable of navigating them and must escape them at all costs. Over time, your efforts to avoid them cause you to deprive yourself of opportunities to live a fulfilled life consistent with your personal values. The price of avoiding your discomfort becomes far greater than the discomfort itself.

You are also aware that the true measure of a boundary's success is being able to consistently maintain your boundary over time and the extent to which you are able to walk away from the situation feeling more grounded, empowered, and in control of your actions. When the purpose of your boundary is to change another person's behavior, make them recognize their unhealthy patterns, gain their understanding, or have them apologize for the hurt they caused, you place the outcome of your boundary entirely in their hands. You give up control over the success of your boundary and set yourself up for disappointment. If, however, your boundary does happen to lead the other person to gain insight, take accountability, or even offer a sincere apology, consider that a bonus, not the objective.

In addition, any boundary you set solely to keep the peace or avoid feeling bad—rather than to foster self-empowerment and inner peace that is not dependent on someone else's mood—may feel like a success in the moment, but over time, it is likely to make you feel increasingly worse and more desperate to maintain the illusion of peace.

When boundaries are grounded in anything other than strengthening your own ability to walk away feeling empowered, they often reinforce the very powerlessness created by narcissistic abuse and coercive control. For survivors, this means boundaries can subtly become yet another tool of self-abandonment rather than self-protection. Rather than strengthening survivors' sense of agency, these boundaries keep their sense of safety, perception of reality, and self-identity entangled with the narcissist, unintentionally giving their abuser control over the survivor's narrative.

Boundaries Based on Old Patterns

As we learned, the behavioral patterns that once worked quite well for you during childhood may no longer be effective. Still, swapping unhealthy familiarity for something unknown can be frightening, even when that change will enhance your life. Even if you can plainly see that your ineffective patterns are holding you back, interfering with your relationships, and causing emotional pain, they can still *feel* safe to you. Over time, you learn to rely on patterns that are keeping you stuck, increasing the risk of relationship difficulties, anxiety, depression, and an overall sense of dissatisfaction. In doing so, you deprive yourself the opportunity to see that you *can* tolerate your internal pain without falling apart.

This can be particularly disempowering for survivors of narcissistic abuse, especially because the patterns being repeated in these dynamics have been deeply engrained over the years. The strategies that once helped you navigate your world as a child, such as staying silent, people-pleasing, overexplaining, or suppressing your own needs, operate automatically. They are simply "how relationships work."

When you shape your boundaries not by the realities of the present situation but by now-ineffective coping strategies from childhood, it is unlikely to produce the outcomes you want. Instead, these boundaries can reinforce the belief that you lack the ability to protect your peace or feel in control within your relationships. Over time, this can erode your self-confidence and cause frustration and hopelessness, as you begin to believe that nothing you do works—so why try at all?

You may also believe that you are navigating the relationship as best you can, but in reality, these interpersonal styles are exactly what the narcissistic dynamic reinforces. You are repeatedly given the message that self-silencing is necessary, that your needs are irrelevant, and that your worth and identity are directly tied to adapting to the narcissist's narrative.

Over the years, many of my clients have expressed the same painful realization, that one of the most devastating aspects of their relationship was that they genuinely believed they were doing the "right" thing. They thought if they just tried harder to adapt, communicated better, or increased their efforts to keep the peace at the expense of their own needs, the relationship would get better and the abuse would stop—but it never did. Sound familiar? If so, it is imperative to understand that this is not a failure or a personal flaw on your part. You just didn't have the support, resources, or mindset to recognize that your patterns of behavior were based on your need for survival, not on living a life consistent with your values. You did—and are doing—the best you could with what you knew and the resources you had at the time.

Boundaries You Can't Maintain

There are several reasons people struggle to maintain boundaries. These can include a lack of social support, pushback from others in the form of peer pressure or guilt trips, financial pressure like being unable to leave a verbally abusive boss, lack of mental health resources, daily stress, and unexpected life events, such as a death in the family that forces interaction with relatives you have gone no contact with.

But as we discussed, consistency is one of the most important aspects of boundary setting. Lax or intermittent boundaries not only create more confusion and chaos in a relationship, but they inadvertently increase the frequency and intensity of the exact behavior you are trying to protect yourself from. In a narcissistic dynamic, the narcissist will exploit your inconsistent boundary, using it as another manipulative tool to test limits and as an opportunity to escalate and intensify their control efforts. You may end up experiencing even more anxiety, self-blame, and doubt, further reinforcing your belief that setting boundaries will never work.

For that reason, the most important question to consider when setting your boundaries within a narcissistic abusive relationship is "Can I maintain this boundary 100 percent of the time?" In other words, what is the likelihood that you can keep doing what the boundary asks you to do, even in the face of pushback and heightened emotional states? If the answer is *unlikely*, it doesn't mean you are incapable of setting a boundary; it simply means your boundary is too psychologically, physically, and even practically difficult in the moment. Setting a new boundary within the context of a narcissistic dynamic, especially one that may be long overdue, is scary and overwhelming. Even when it's the "right" thing to do and something you truly want to implement, making immediate changes can often feel impossible for you in the moment. That's why starting small can be such a powerful strategy. I always advise my patients to start with what I refer to as "insultingly small steps." In other words, break your boundary down into such tiny concrete components that each one feels almost pointless. Tackling a boundary from this approach incrementally increases your confidence in your ability to maintain the boundary consistently over time. But that's not all—consistency is also a key factor in making the boundary a habit. The more consistent a behavior, the more comfortable it becomes for you, and the easier it is to maintain, even with all of life's challenges and distractions.

It is important to clarify that adjustments to your boundaries should be based on changes in circumstances, not on fear, avoidance, or uncertainty. If a larger boundary feels too big right now, whether because of financial resources or lack of social and emotional support, that is completely okay. You can always adjust your boundaries over time. You can choose to take on more as you gain strength or scale them back if circumstances call for it. When done mindfully, flexible boundaries allow you to protect your peace while remaining true to yourself, safely moving you forward, step by step.

Keep in mind, setting a big boundary all at once does not equal bigger and better results. It won't shock the narcissist into changing or get them to suddenly take accountability for their hurtful actions. What it *can* do, however, is increase the risk for inconsistency and self-doubt. Starting small and appropriately modifying when needed does not diminish your boundary's power; it makes it sustainable, values-driven, and authentically you.

For example, imagine you receive news that your favorite uncle has passed away. You plan to attend his funeral, but doing so means you will see your mother, with whom you've been no contact for three years. You'll be in her company all week at family dinners and gatherings, where she will almost certainly try to start conversations. In this situation, it may feel most appropriate for you to interact with her and simply keep it brief—say hello, be civil, and walk away rather than engaging in lengthy discussions or ignoring her altogether. This does not mean you are setting inconsistent boundaries, avoiding discomfort, or acting against your values. You are simply adjusting your boundary to fit what *you* feel is appropriate for the circumstance while still honoring your needs and limits. Avoiding the funeral (and avoiding the discomfort of seeing your mom) would take you away from what matters most to you in the moment—honoring your uncle.

As you go through the process of identifying, breaking down, and implementing boundaries, it is important to give yourself grace if you are not able to follow the rigid (and often unrealistic) "strong boundaries, zero tolerance" advice that is often thrown around in social media posts. Not being able to set a huge boundary right out of the gate within any dynamic, but particularly within a narcissistic abusive relationship, does not mean you are weak, unworthy, or incapable. Setting and maintaining boundaries with a narcissist is a challenging, unfamiliar, and often scary behavior change. It is perfectly normal to need time, practice, and adjustments to find what actually works for you. You will find yourself in various types of situations, and your boundaries may look different depending on circumstances (e.g., wedding, work event, unexpected encounter, holiday season, following a recent breakup). Adjust your boundaries as needed, being sure changes are not driven solely by emotional avoidance and that they continue to support, rather than undermine, what you truly value.

EXERCISE: Boundary Breakdown

This exercise will help you learn how to break down difficult or daunting boundaries into more manageable components.

List some of the boundaries you have been implementing or would like to implement within an existing unhealthy relationship. Then rate these boundaries based on three criteria:

- On a scale of 1–5, rate each boundary on its maintainability, with 1 being easy to maintain and 5 being very difficult to maintain.
- On a scale of 1–5, rate each boundary on how much time and energy it takes to maintain it, with 1 being none and 5 being a great deal.
- On a scale of 1–5, rate each boundary on its effectiveness, with 1 being not effective at all and 5 being extremely effective.

Boundary	Maintainability	Time and Energy	Effectiveness

What do you notice about your ratings?

____

____

____

Which boundary is the most difficult to maintain? Why?

____

____

____

Would this boundary be more effective if you broke it down into more manageable components? Why?

____

____

____

How might you break this boundary down into smaller, more manageable elements?

____

____

____

The Ripple Effect of Boundaries

Every relationship has a "dance"—that is, a pattern of interpersonal behaviors that have formed over the course of the relationship and that serves as the blueprint for most or all interactions. Think for a moment about your own relationships with various people. There's a good chance that you can predict each person's responses to anything you might do or say based on your history with them.

While you can't directly control another person's behavior within this dance, you can throw them off step by changing even just the smallest aspect of your own behavior. It can be extremely empowering to see how shifting your own behavior, such as setting a boundary, can indirectly influence another's actions. The following example demonstrates how you can influence the relationship dance by slightly shifting your own boundaries.

Lauren and William have been living together as a couple for five years. Their relationship has always been healthy, with the occasional relationship hiccups. However, in the last year, the couple has not been getting along and there is a notable tension between them.

Their arguments follow a very specific pattern: Lauren accuses William of being dismissive of her feelings, while he thinks Lauren constantly picks on him; he feels as though nothing he does is right. To avoid an argument, Lauren finds it easier to shut down and keep her feelings to herself in the moment. Since she was a child, Lauren has had a pattern of pushing down her emotions until she can no longer contain them, resulting in seemingly random outbursts of anger. William has difficulty making sense of Lauren's disproportionate reactions and becomes overwhelmed with confusion as to why she's suddenly so angry at him. The couple will typically argue back and forth without resolution, ending with Lauren running upstairs and locking herself in their bedroom and William storming out of the house. The next morning, William always tries to put the argument behind them, while Lauren remains upset and accuses him of being insensitive to her feelings.

Once you understand the unique blueprint of a relationship's dance, you begin to see how each person's behavior influences the other's—and from that awareness, we can shift our actions with intention to create healthier outcome for ourselves. With this idea in mind, let's look at the framework of this couple's dance.

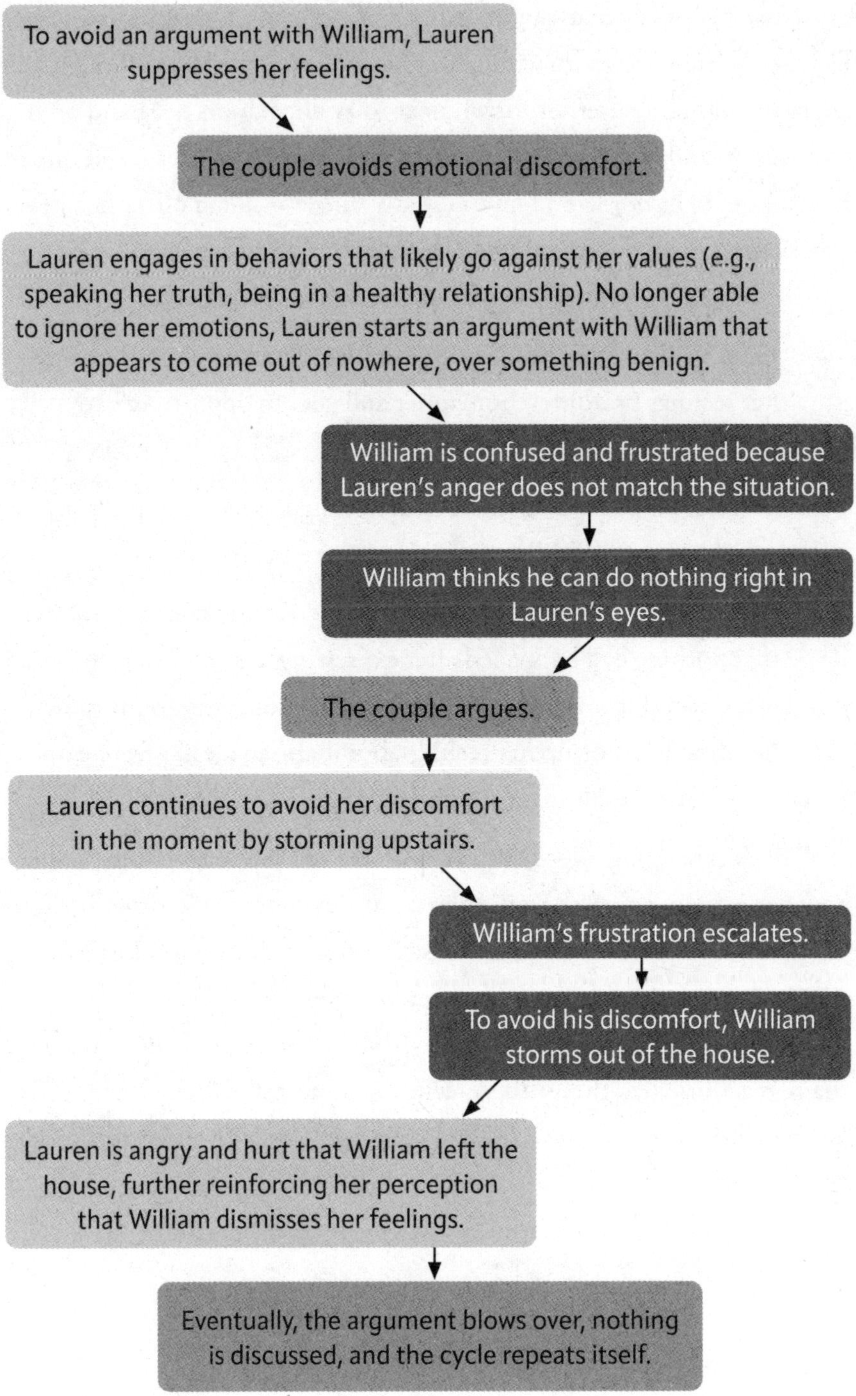
To avoid an argument with William, Lauren suppresses her feelings.
The couple avoids emotional discomfort.
Lauren engages in behaviors that likely go against her values (e.g., speaking her truth, being in a healthy relationship). No longer able to ignore her emotions, Lauren starts an argument with William that appears to come out of nowhere, over something benign.
William is confused and frustrated because Lauren's anger does not match the situation.
William thinks he can do nothing right in Lauren's eyes.
The couple argues.
Lauren continues to avoid her discomfort in the moment by storming upstairs.
William's frustration escalates.
To avoid his discomfort, William storms out of the house.
Lauren is angry and hurt that William left the house, further reinforcing her perception that William dismisses her feelings.
Eventually, the argument blows over, nothing is discussed, and the cycle repeats itself.

Now consider what might happen if, instead of pushing away her feelings, Lauren was more willing to tolerate her discomfort. Though still angry and upset, Lauren sits down next to William, puts her hand on his, and calmly and directly expresses her emotions in that exact moment. Her shift in behavior would undoubtedly throw William off, as he's never experienced Lauren responding in this way during an argument.

By indirectly pushing him off balance, a few things occur:

- First, William has the new experience of Lauren communicating her feelings in a different manner and gets an opportunity to respond to her in real time.
- Second, his confusion about Lauren's anger is cleared up, since he now knows specifically what upset her in the first place.
- Lastly, Lauren gives herself a new experience that confirms for her that nothing bad happened after expressing her emotions. In fact, just the opposite occurred. Expressing her concerns not only kept her from bottling up her feelings, but it also made her feel heard and did not result in an argument.

While changing old patterns will be an ongoing effort, Lauren now has evidence that she can tolerate an uncomfortable situation, and William no longer has a reason to storm out of the house. Instead, the couple shares a nice dinner they cooked together.

By changing just one behavior within their dance, Lauren set up a chain reaction that threw the entire dynamic off balance, launched a much healthier dance, and gave her a sense of control over what typically felt like chaos.

REFLECTION

Consider your relational dance with someone. What patterns emerge? Describe or draw this cycle in the following space.

What is one step in your dance that you are willing to shift? This could be an actual behavior, your tone of voice, your word choice, or even changing an element of your body language.

Once you have tested out your behavior adjustment, map or describe what you observed in the following space. Were there differences in how the dance played out?

Did you feel an initial increase in internal discomfort when shifting your behaviors?

What did you do with this discomfort? Did you allow it to prevent you from making a shift?

What did you notice happened to your discomfort *after* shifting your behavior?

How did the other person in your dance initially respond to your shift?

Explain the chain reaction that resulted from changing this single behavior.

Which behaviors in the other person were indirectly influenced by your intentional shift?

In the past, have you ever attempted to directly change or modify the behaviors of the other person in your dance? Were your efforts successful?

Do you find more discomfort in trying to change someone else's behavior directly or adjusting your own responses in ways that allow the interaction to unfold differently? Why?

When Boundaries Meet Pushback

When one person in a relationship dynamic makes even the tiniest behavior shift, everyone in that system loses their footing, even if they are not directly impacted. Humans are creatures of habit and change makes us uncomfortable. Even if the change is for the best, we can feel uncertain, anxious, and even downright scared. To avoid this discomfort, people will often push back against change in hopes of restoring the familiarity of the original dynamic—even if it's unhealthy.

We see this pattern play out within all kinds of relational systems. A mother begins refusing to do her teenagers' laundry anymore, and the kids threaten not to go to school because they have "nothing to wear." A friend stops participating in conversations where the group gossips about whoever isn't there, only to be told they aren't fun to be around anymore. Pushback from others can be difficult to navigate, but if you continue to hold your boundary, it becomes more likely that, over time, others will shift their behaviors in response to yours. The teenagers eventually start doing their own laundry; the friend group comes to realize that gossiping about each other is driving them apart; in general, the entire system adjusts to accommodate your behavior shifts.

In a narcissistic relationship, however, pushback is more than just returning to the status quo. The more values-aligned your behaviors become, the less control the narcissist has, and the harder they will try to manipulate you back into your old patterns. Passive-aggressive comments and cutting jokes may turn into full-blown insults and outlandish accusations. Intimidation tactics like getting in your personal space or blocking your exit from a room may progress to throwing things, destroying your personal property, or even physically assaulting you. This is also where we tend to see many of the hoovering behaviors discussed in chapter 2, including smear campaigns or flying monkeys, which enlist other people in the effort to draw you back into the abuse cycle.

Those outside your relationship likely don't understand the true nature and extent of the narcissistic abuse you are experiencing; to them, an unhealthy status quo may seem a better option than uncomfortable change.

The following example illustrates what can happen in these dynamics when a survivor disrupts the status quo by engaging in more values-driven behaviors and establishing healthy boundaries.

Since Eric was a child, his mother, Bonnie, had placed extremely high demands on him and held him to exceptionally high standards. This was evident in almost every domain of Eric's life, including academics, sports, and his social life. When Eric was unable to meet these unrelenting standards, his mother would berate and shame him, calling him a "loser" and "an embarrassment to the family." It was not uncommon for Bonnie to ignore him for days at a time if he failed to meet her demands in any way. Any attempt by Eric to think independently or focus on his own interests was met with harsh criticism, shame, verbal abuse, and even threats of withdrawing all financial support. Bonnie often used guilt to punish Eric, routinely reminding him of how much she had sacrificed for him over the years and insisting he show respect by acknowledging that. From an early age, Eric absorbed the message that meeting his mother's expectations and lofty demands were the debt he owed her for the sacrifices she made.

His brother, Scott, did not experience the same relationship with their mother. Scott was treated as the "golden child" who could do no wrong. There were very few consequences or rules placed on Scott. While Scott acknowledged that he and his brother were treated very differently, there wasn't much support he could offer Eric beyond sympathy and advice to "just don't let her push you around so much."

Eric's father, Jack, took a passive stance in the family dynamic. He worked late hours and kept himself removed from day-to-day family interactions. When he was within earshot of the emotionally heightened interactions between Eric and Bonnie, his only response was "Eric, apologize to your mother." Any time Eric tried to communicate his frustrations to his father, he was met with invalidating statements such as "You know how your mother is" and "Just do what she says so she doesn't get angry."

Bonnie's harsh criticism and demands continued as Eric reached adulthood and attempted to establish his own life. She would show up at his house uninvited, and when Eric asked her to leave, she would become enraged at his "ingratitude." Bonnie disapproved of Eric's girlfriend, Sherie, and accused her of deliberately drawing a wedge between Eric and his family. Through the years, however, Eric had come to realize the impact of his mother's manipulation and toxic behaviors. When he and Sherie got engaged, they decided it was necessary to implement boundaries with Eric's mother so that their marriage wouldn't suffer, including:

- Bonnie cannot show up unannounced to their house.
- All communication from Bonnie must be in writing.

- All text messages and emails from Bonnie must include both Eric and Sherie so they present as a unified front to prevent splitting and manipulation.
- All of Bonnie's manipulative comments and actions would be ignored.

As expected, Bonnie did not respond well to these boundaries. In fact, she disregarded them altogether and became increasingly irate. However, the couple remained consistent with their boundaries. Because Bonnie now had considerably less control over Eric and was unable to penetrate his boundaries, she began directing her focus and anger toward her husband. Unaccustomed to direct conflict with his wife, Jack contacted Eric, pleading with him to call his mother and make amends. When Eric gently refused, continuing to maintain his boundaries, Jack became even more emotionally disconnected from the family, working later hours and even going to the office on weekends. With limited access to Eric, and now Jack, Bonnie shifted her attention once again, but this time to Scott, the "favorite child." She began reaching out to Scott more often, keeping him on the phone for hours while she complained about Eric and Jack, and then, when she ran out of complaints, asking increasingly critical and very personal questions about Scott's professional, social, and romantic life.

Having never been the target of his mother's passive-aggressive behavior and harsh remarks, Scott took Eric to task for upsetting their mom and insisted that he apologize to her. When Eric refused to do so, Scott became furious. While Scott recognized that the relationship between Eric and their mother was unhealthy, he was more interested in keeping his position as the golden child than in supporting his brother's efforts to establish healthy boundaries.

As we see in this example, a narcissist's manipulative narrative and controlling behaviors are often enabled by those around them, either knowingly or unknowingly. Even people who sincerely believe they are helping the situation, who have no malicious intent, can unintentionally perpetuate the abusive cycle. When Eric's boundaries prohibited his mom from obtaining supply, she focused her control efforts on other family members, a dynamic they had never directly experienced with her. This created considerable discomfort within these other family members, which they quickly sought to extinguish by pushing Eric to drop his boundaries and return to the family's status quo—not because it was healthier, but because it was familiar and where they felt most comfortable.

As you become increasingly more confident in setting and maintaining boundaries with the narcissist in your life, it is important to remember that, while these are necessary steps toward healing, they are not easy. Shifting your boundaries, no matter how big or small, can bring about intense feelings of shame, fear, and guilt, especially when you are met with repeated pushback from family, friends, and anyone the narcissist has enlisted in their campaign to regain control, influence, and power over you. Often, discomfort is actually a key indicator that your boundaries are working. The difficult emotions that arise when setting boundaries with a narcissist simply mean you are doing something *different*—something that, until now, you have likely avoided *because it felt so uncomfortable.* In other words, if you feel scared, guilty, and incredibly anxious, you're probably doing the right thing.

How to Handle Pushback

Sometimes it's possible to approach the narcissist's pushback with nonreactivity (e.g., ignoring text messages, responding to insults with indifference, avoiding interactions with them). But there may be instances where these types of responses are not applicable and an alternative type of response is necessary. For example, imagine you are an adult child of a narcissistic parent. They leave you a voicemail saying "Do you still want your high school photo albums? I guess if you can't come get them today, I'll put them out on the curb for garbage day." You understand your parent's threat to throw away the albums is a manipulative tactic to provoke you—to start an argument or cause a sudden inconvenience in your schedule. But, if the albums are of great importance to you and hold sentimental value, you may feel compelled to respond. The key, however, is to respond with emotional neutrality rather than a heightened reaction, such as arguing with your parent or getting into a lengthy debate about how they are inconsiderate. Emotional neutrality includes the words you use, tone of voice, and body language. Sitting with your feelings while responding in a way that does not give your parent the supply they are seeking gives you a feeling of increased control.

One specific type of nonreactive response is known as *gray rocking*. It is a deliberate and consistent strategy that goes beyond simply being emotionally neutral. Instead, you adopt an ongoing behavioral pattern designed to come across as completely unengaging and dull in every interaction with the narcissist. It is a boundary that safeguards your emotional energy by denying the narcissist any reaction of engagement, gradually leaving them with nothing to feed on. Over time, the absence of supply leads the narcissist to lose interest, giving you breathing room, inner peace, and space to regain control over your personal narrative.

The following example demonstrates what happens within a narcissistic abusive dynamic when you apply the gray rocking method.

Carolyn and Amy were first cousins. Despite Amy's unpredictable moods and demanding nature, Carolyn had always been a source of support for Amy, often at the expense of her own needs. She always felt the need to walk on eggshells around Amy, never knowing what could set her off. Amy was extremely possessive of their relationship and would become angry if not included in Carolyn's plans.

On one occasion, Carolyn asked her own mother to accompany her for support to her breast biopsy appointment. Amy became so enraged at Carolyn for not asking her to come that not only did she neglect to ask about the biopsy results, but she refused to speak to Carolyn for months.

When Carolyn unfortunately received her breast cancer diagnosis, Amy was less than supportive. She completely ghosted Carolyn while she underwent chemotherapy, leaving her to wonder what she had done wrong for Amy to have cut her off. During this time, Amy started posting passive-aggressive quotes on social media about "always putting family first" and "knowing who your real friends are." Carolyn was devastated. As her health improved, however, her devastation and confusion turned into anger, and she decided to block Amy on social media. The time away from Amy, while navigating her illness, had given her clarity into the toxic nature of their relationship. Carolyn knew that expressing her anger and frustration to Amy would never end in any sort of healthy resolution. Years of being in this toxic dynamic had shown her that Amy would never take accountability for her behaviors.

It wasn't more than 24 hours after blocking her that Amy sent a text asking Carolyn how she was feeling. In the past, Carolyn would have immediately reengaged and kept her feelings to herself out of fear of upsetting Amy. She thought about ignoring the text, and even considered going no contact, but family functions and holidays would make that boundary too difficult to adhere to consistently. So, Carolyn simply responded with "I'm fine, thank you."

Amy: "Let's get coffee tomorrow!"

Carolyn: "I have plans."

Amy: "Why wouldn't you want to see me after all this time? I see you haven't changed at all. You're still just as selfish. I don't know why I bothered checking in to see how you're feeling."

Carolyn: "Thanks for checking in."

Amy continued to send lengthy, accusatory, and berating texts, but Carolyn was no longer responding.

Several weeks later, they both attended the same family wedding. After the ceremony, Amy immediately approached Carolyn and greeted her with a hug and kiss as if nothing had happened. Rather than appearing defensive or upset or reverting to her quick-to-forgive pattern, Carolyn simply said hello in a neutral tone of voice and calmly walked away. Enraged, Amy stormed after Carolyn, screaming at her for being self-absorbed. With the exact same tone as before, Carolyn responded, "We will just have to disagree on that." She then sat down at her table and began a conversation with the guest seated next to her until eventually, Amy walked away.

Notice how Carolyn didn't raise her voice, didn't become outwardly emotional, and didn't reengage in a back-and-forth with Amy. Despite her own feelings of anger, Carolyn's tone stayed level, her body language neutral, and her responses short, fact-based, and absent of emotion and personal opinions. She wasn't cruel, just completely unengaging. By gray rocking, she protected her energy, successfully managed her emotions and behaviors, and made it clear she was no longer available for the push-pull dynamic that Amy thrived on.

It is important to recognize that at no point did Carolyn make a direct effort to change Amy's behavior. Rather, she changed her own response to Amy's toxic behavior, and most importantly, she maintained this change regardless of what Amy threw her way. Her short, simple, non-emotional responses gave Amy nothing to grab hold of, depriving her of the supply she was craving.

Guidelines for Gray Rocking

If conversation with the narcissist is inevitable, it is always best to use as few words as possible; refrain from lengthy explanations, rationalizations, and arguments; and respond with facts only, never emotions or opinions. In addition, it is always best to have all communication in writing if possible. This is particularly useful for work-related issues, coparenting, and cases where gaslighting is frequently used as a manipulation tactic.

EXERCISE: Text Tactics

In the space provided, write down what you believe to be a neutral, gray rock response to the following text messages sent by a narcissistic abuser.

"Did you forget your meds? I don't want you around our daughter acting crazy. You are an unstable mother, and everyone knows it. You only care about yourself and are a danger to our child. We are having a long conversation about your mental stability and your capabilities as a parent when I come to pick my kid up tonight for my weekend."

Response:

____

____

____

____

"After all I've done for you, this is how you repay me? By going to your in-laws for Thanksgiving? Every son I know goes to their own mother's house for Thanksgiving. I don't deserve this type of treatment. Ever since you got married, your wife has done nothing but try to put a wedge between us. I feel like I don't even recognize you anymore. This is not the son I raised."

Response:

____

____

____

____

"Why can't you just let it go? You're so sensitive. How can we make this relationship work if you won't even give me another chance? Everyone makes mistakes! You're far from perfect. Plus, that's not even what happened! You make these crazy stories up in your head and then accuse me of crap I never did! You need therapy!"

Response:

____

____

____

____

"All you do is ask me for money. Don't you know how to budget? I give you plenty. I don't care what the court agreement says; I'm not paying $200 for health insurance for our kid. Why don't you try to find a job that pays you more, since you claim to care about our kid so much? You're pathetic."

Response:

____

____

____

____

Navigating Setbacks

Boundary setting is not an easy process. Setbacks are normal and expected. Most importantly, they do not equate to failure. In fact, setbacks allow us to regroup and reassess our situation so that we become even more confident and more successful moving forward. This is an extremely important consideration for those in relationships with a narcissistic abuser. For example, it takes on average seven attempts for someone to leave an abusive relationship for good.* Many survivors who go back to their abuser experience tremendous feelings of failure, confusion, shame, and guilt, and the confidence in their ability to leave for good is shaken. They may become even more withdrawn, feeling embarrassed to confide in friends and family after returning to the relationship. What so many

* Sarah M. Buel, "50 Obstacles to Leaving," National Domestic Violence Hotline, https://www.thehotline.org/resources/get-help-50-obstacles-to-leaving.

survivors don't realize, however, is that this back-and-forth is *not* a sign of weakness or failure. Each time they leave and return, they are one step closer to leaving for good.

Setbacks are an expected and necessary part of growth and healing. You need to give yourself grace during this difficult time—perfection is not a realistic or healthy goal, especially when your physical safety is a primary concern. Rather, the goal is being able to acknowledge when you've strayed from your boundary, reflecting on what went wrong, making the necessary adjustments, and recommitting rather than giving up entirely or telling yourself "I can't do this." When understood as a normal part of the boundary-setting process, setbacks can be a powerful way of propelling you forward to healing and, ultimately, escaping from the abuse.

REFLECTION

Describe a time in your relationship when a boundary became too difficult to maintain.

____

____

____

____

Did you view this as a setback? How did it make you feel about yourself and your situation?

____

____

____

____

After the setback, were you able to recover and recommit to your boundary? Explain.

____

____

____

____

Conclusion

Change is hard and uncomfortable. Our brains naturally crave structure and routine. For this reason, people will often gravitate toward what is familiar rather than what may be healthier; it simply feels safer and easier. This can make it difficult to create and maintain purposeful and values-driven boundaries—it may mean giving up behaviors that have been part of our daily life for years or allowing ourselves to experience painful and scary emotions we typically work so hard to avoid. But it's also precisely why setting a new boundary can be so transformative.

As you now know, the goal of a boundary is not to directly change a narcissist's abusive behavior, but to protect your mental wellness, define for yourself what you are and are not willing to tolerate, and help you regain a sense of control within the chaos. Therefore, the best indicator for determining the efficacy of a boundary is the degree to which it helps you regulate your internal experiences, not only during direct interactions with the narcissist but also when their influence continues to affect you—even when they are physically absent or long after the relationship ends. If you're able to regulate your internal experiences, remain aligned with your values, and walk away feeling at peace and empowered, that is a clear sign your boundaries have worked!

If you find yourself having difficulty consistently maintaining your boundaries with the narcissist, it's vital to remember that getting tangled up in the surface details of their behaviors and words is a futile cycle. Any attempt at meaningful engagement only serves to fill their supply and increase their control, power, and influence over you. Once you can become an active observer of the narcissist's patterns and are able to predict their behavior and respond with neutrality, you will know your boundary has been effective. The confidence gained in maintaining successful boundaries is a significant step forward in the healing journey.

5

Narcissistic Abuse Outside of Intimate Relationships

One of the defining features of NPD is that it manifests as a pervasive personality style, meaning it presents within all domains of a narcissist's life. Far from being limited to their romantic and intimate relationships, it extends deep into their relationships with immediate and extended family, colleagues, friends, neighbors, and even complete strangers. But while the underlying function of the narcissist's abuse remains consistent across relationships, the way it manifests will differ based on the specific dynamic and the narcissist's needs at any given moment. This chapter will offer you a framework to identify narcissistic abuse across a variety of different relationships and provide protective strategies to use when you are faced with the narcissist's coercive control and abuse.

Narcissistic Parents

Unlike having a narcissistic partner, with whom you have a clear before-and-after sense of self-identity, being raised by a narcissistic parent leaves no point of reference for who you were before the abuse. Instead, your narrative is created at birth by the narcissistic parent's agenda and is continuously reinforced throughout your life through their control over your choices and behaviors. Needless to say, this insidious abuse has a profound impact on your development and can permeate your relationships throughout your life.

The primary way a narcissistic parent maintains power over their child is by preventing them from developing a core sense of self and punishing any attempt at individuality. Rather than seeing their children as unique individuals with their own feelings, perceptions, interests, and opinions, a narcissistic parent often sees their children as possessions and direct extensions of themself. In the eyes of the parent, you exist only to the extent that you can meet their needs at any given moment. The narcissistic parent conditions you to believe that you are responsible for their emotions, that you are the cause of their behaviors, and that you must prioritize their needs at the expense of your own. In general, the more you comply with their narrative, the safer you feel and the more affection you receive. But inevitably, the narcissistic parent will suddenly yet deliberately change the rules of the relationship without explanation, leaving you confused and desperate to understand what you did wrong. This vicious loop of closeness and coldness, acceptance and shame, keeps you locked in a dysfunctional cycle, making it increasingly easier for the narcissistic parent to maintain their controlling grasp on you.

A narcissistic parent views any steps you take toward autonomy as abandonment, disrespect, or disloyalty. These steps may range from something as minor as expressing independent views or opinions to natural maturation milestones, like graduating from high school, moving out of the house, getting married, or having children of your own. The more independent you become, the more the narcissistic parent feels their control slipping, which results in an increase in manipulative and abusive behaviors.

How Narcissistic Parenting Shows Up in the Family

While every family has its own story, those raised by narcissistic parents often experience strikingly similar patterns that reflect the blueprint of narcissistic abuse:

- You are taught from an early age that the narcissistic parent's love and attention is contingent on how well you meet their needs and live in accordance with their narrative. If you meet the parent's needs, you are seen as good; if you don't, you are deemed bad. This dichotomous perception is reinforced by arbitrary standards that can change without notice. As a result, you are never able to satisfy the needs of your parent and are conditioned to believe a false narrative that nothing you do will ever be good enough and that you are unworthy of being loved.
- Narcissistic parents go about obtaining power and control with the same range of abusive behaviors we've discussed previously. They may use love bombing in the form of extravagant gifts, financial support, favoritism, and praise. They may trigger emotions like guilt, blame, and fear through the silent treatment, intimidation, or threats of abandonment or physical abuse. Another way to gain control over you is by being the primary owner of family information. In other words, they deliberately pick and choose what information to share with each child, often resulting in siblings being pitted against one another. Narcissistic parents will also gaslight you throughout your development, making you doubt your own perceptions and memories from an early age, ensuring that you remain dependent upon the parent. For example, a narcissistic parent may deny your experience of abuse, insisting that you are lying or making trouble. Future faking is another common tactic used by narcissistic parents to manipulate

and control your emotions: The parent repeatedly gives you false hope by deliberately promising something they have no intention of delivering. When it isn't fulfilled, the parent blames you, leaving you confused, disappointed, and doubting yourself, all to manipulate your mood and to increase dependence on the parent.

- Some narcissistic parents are neglectful caregivers, ignoring your basic needs, such as adequate food, clothing, medical care, or emotional support, but portraying the image of an attentive parent in public. They may deliberately dismiss important milestones like birthdays or deny you recognition for academic or athletic success. In some cases, they may even provide food, clothing, or supervision selectively, ensuring these needs are met for themselves or other family members but withholding them from you. This neglect is not accidental—not only is it used as a control tactic, but it also reflects the parent's belief that performing such responsibilities are unnecessary since they do not benefit the parent personally.
- Other narcissistic parents take the opposite approach, becoming excessively involved in every aspect of your life. They may do things like dictate your friendships, override your ability to make your own decisions, and deny you any sense of privacy. When you seek independence or personal space, your parent interprets it as rejection and accuses you of being ungrateful or unloving after "everything they have sacrificed for you" or claims that you are punishing them for "loving you too much." The parent treats your life choices and privacy as something owed to them.
- Many narcissistic parents present an entirely different parenting persona in public. Around others, they will appear attentive, nurturing, and even doting, with the goal of projecting the image of an ideal parent. This contrast can create immense confusion, shame, and embarrassment for you. If the parent has the

capability to act appropriately in some contexts, you assume the mistreatment behind closed doors must be your fault. Over time, this reinforces self-blame and unworthiness while strengthening the parent's control, keeping you locked in the abuse cycle and unsure of your own reality and self-image.

While there is overlap between how these patterns show up in mothers versus fathers, it is important to note the differences as well. Keep in mind, regardless of how abusive behavior manifests, the function of the behaviors remains the same—to maintain control, power, and dominance over the child. This may be due to myriad factors, including gender roles, the dynamics specific to each family, and social expectations.

Mothers

A narcissistic mother may oscillate between overbearing and enmeshed to absent and neglectful, deliberately creating a pattern of emotional dependency within you. A narcissistic mother is likely to demand constant validation from you, using guilt and shame to emotionally manipulate you into meeting her needs. She insists that you perpetually owe her for the sacrifices she has made as a mother, while simultaneously reinforcing the false belief that nothing you do will ever be enough to satisfy her needs. In short, the mother sets a transactional tone in her relationship with her child, with her personal narrative as currency.

It is not uncommon for a narcissistic mother to view her child, especially a daughter, as competition. Because she views you as a direct extension of herself, almost as if you are an accessory, your individual opinions and interests are frequently invalidated, ignored, or punished. A narcissistic mother may see your success or appearance as a threat and undermine you through manipulative tactics and sabotage, or she may take credit for your achievements, again reinforcing her narrative that you must depend on her for validation, success, and safety.

Fathers

Narcissistic fathers tend to be more overtly domineering, authoritarian, emotionally disconnected, and increasingly absent from your day-to-day life. Narcissistic fathers often instill chronic feelings of inadequacy in you, due to their excessive criticism and lofty standards, and project their own shortcomings onto you to avoid accountability. They may command constant admiration and brag about their own achievements (or take ownership of yours) while belittling and trivializing your personal efforts.

While both narcissistic mothers and fathers can be physically abusive, fathers do present as more physically aggressive and use fear and intimidation to enforce their control. However, narcissistic fathers will sometimes adopt a victim role, presenting as martyrs. This is common post-separation, particularly when custody issues are present.

Just as narcissistic mothers are often jealous of their daughters, fathers often view their sons as competition and will either seek to sabotage their successes in life or take full ownership of their accomplishments. This can include academic achievements, athletics, and even social relationships. No matter how successful or high-achieving you may be, it will never be good enough for a narcissistic father. This can result in a never-ending cycle where the narcissistic father constantly devalues your efforts throughout your life, trapping you in an endless struggle of seeking approval.

Common Controlling Behaviors

The following list includes examples of coercively controlling behaviors commonly displayed by narcissistic parents within the family:

- Making you feel that you owe them for all the sacrifices they made to raise you
- Pitting siblings against one another

- Acting emotionally hot and cold without reason, leaving you to wonder what you did wrong (e.g., giving you the silent treatment)
- Arbitrarily withholding attention and affection to punish you and manipulate you into engaging in certain behavior
- Strategically withholding information (e.g., the correct time of a family event, illness of a family member) to damage your credibility and control how others perceive you as well as how you perceive yourself
- Taking credit for your achievements and accolades
- Refusing any accountability for their role in the fractured relationship with you
- Using finances (e.g., threatening to leave you out of their will) to coerce you into engaging in a particular behavior or to instill feelings of fear and guilt
- Threatening to expose personal information or embarrassing stories about you
- Using the emotions of guilt and shame to manipulate and coerce you
- Blaming you for family chaos and dysfunction
- Body/weight shaming you
- Repeatedly violating your privacy with the sole purpose of stripping you of your autonomy and to assert dominance rather than as a response to appropriate safety concerns
- Sabotaging your social and intimate relationships by routinely overstepping boundaries, gaslighting, and instilling guilt and shame for your choices (e.g., "Why do you always date such losers?")
- Being unsupportive of your gifts and talents, except when it benefits the parent directly, such as highlighting your successes in public

- Critiquing your parenting abilities, as it pertains to the grandchildren
- Being unsupportive of you when you have physical or mental health difficulties (e.g., blaming, mocking, minimizing, or ignoring your struggles altogether)
- Repeatedly causing chaos on important and meaningful dates, such as birthdays, graduations, and weddings
- Badmouthing other family members and forcing you to pick sides or engage in the toxic dialogue
- Discussing topics with you that are inappropriate for your age, including marital issues in the home or the parent's sexual activity

REFLECTION

Circle the behaviors in the previous list that resonate most for you. Then describe a time when these behaviors showed up in your relationship with your parent.

____

____

____

What were/are the underlying functions of these behaviors?

____

____

____

How might your responses to these behaviors change now that you understand the importance of responding to the function of your parent's behavior rather than to their surface-level actions and words?

____

____

____

The following two scenarios illustrate how a narcissistic parent's behavior patterns unfold within family dynamics and highlight the ways in which they obtain control and power over the child while also perpetuating their personal narrative. These examples will help you to identify the behaviors of narcissistic parents and gain a deeper understanding of the impact this form of abuse has not only on the child, but on the entire family system.

Jada and Leonard

Jada was the oldest of two sisters. She had always stood out for her academic achievements, even as a child in elementary school. Jada excelled in science and math throughout her academic career and had decided from an early age that she wanted to become a doctor just like her father, Leonard, who was adored and respected as a physician in the community.

Though outwardly Leonard spoke highly of his daughter and praised her achievements, he frequently took credit for her successes. It was as though her own efforts were irrelevant and existed only to the extent that her father deemed them worthy. If, however, she did not achieve success or meet his expectations, he would blame Jada, claiming she was unintelligent, unmotivated, and an embarrassment to him and the medical community.

Their relationship was largely transactional—the more Jada appeased her father, the more attention and praise she received. However, he held her to relentlessly high standards, which if not achieved, would often result in some form of punishment. Typically, if Leonard was not satisfied with Jada's grades or performance, he would express his disgust through emotionally abusive behavior and other coercively controlling tactics such as silent treatments or verbal abuse. For example, when Jada did not receive the highest grade in her AP physics class, Leonard subsequently withheld all affection, attention, and communication from her as a form of punishment. He would belittle her, saying she would ultimately fail in the medical world and be an embarrassment to the field.

Angelo and Rosa

Angelo and his wife, Emily, were eagerly expecting their first child together. As part of their birth plan, the couple decided that they did not want to have any visitors at the hospital for the first 12 hours following the birth; it was something they both felt strongly about. When Angelo's parents heard of their delivery plan, his mother, Rosa, became furious. She accused the couple of ruining the birth of her first grandchild with their disrespectful and selfish decision. After everything Rosa had sacrificed for her son, she could not fathom why he would agree to exclude her from visiting right after the baby was born. She was so offended that she canceled the baby shower she had planned for Emily and refused to speak to the couple.

A few weeks later, Emily was admitted to the hospital to have the baby. The couple was elated. While waiting for the baby, Angelo received a phone call from his mother. Rosa proceeded to berate him for being a horrible son and ruining this once-in-a-lifetime moment for her as a grandmother. Even after Angelo hung up the phone, she continued to send multiple text messages accusing Emily of breaking apart their family and isolating her grandchild. The text messages continued well into the evening through Emily's delivery of a healthy baby girl. After the couple's 12-hour privacy period, Rosa was the only family member not to come to the hospital.

Answer the following questions based on the two previous case scenarios.

1. What were the manipulative tactics used by Leonard and Rosa?

____

____

____

2. What were the functions of these abuse tactics?

____

____

____

3. Provide a response for each scenario based only on what is being *said* and what can be directly observed. Explain the impact these specific responses would have on the narcissistic parents' behaviors.

____

____

____

____

4. Now, provide a response for each scenario that takes into account the underlying *function* of the narcissistic parents' behaviors.

____

____

____

____

5. Describe the differences between the responses based on words and those based on function in these scenarios.

____

____

____

____

6. What boundaries might be effective in these situations?

____

____

____

____

Narcissistic In-Laws

Sometimes the narcissistic parent isn't your own—it's your partner's. My patients who have a narcissistic in-law describe it as feeling like there's a third person in their relationship, intrusively weighing in on everything from finances and career decisions to parenting advice and even simple activities of daily living. These boundary violations are often driven by the narcissist's perception that they are losing control over their child. When someone commits to a partner, their narcissistic parent experiences a loss of power and often responds with highly intrusive and manipulative efforts to reclaim the control and ownership of their child. The narcissist views the spouse as a threat not only to their control over their child, but also to the narrative they have crafted for their child over their lifetime.

Like the love bombing that occurs within the early stages of a romantic relationship, we often see the same playbook in the early stages of the in-law relationship. While there is variation in how the narcissistic blueprint presents, it's common for parents to initially present as loving, kind, overly generous, and in full support of the union. Much like the idealization stage of a romantic relationship, these behaviors are a strategic form of impression management and quickly establish their role within the relationship, ensuring access to you, as their child's partner. The narcissist appears highly supportive and trustworthy, but this is merely a facade designed to make you feel increasingly more comfortable, allowing the narcissist access to your vulnerabilities, which they will later exploit.

As the relationship progresses and develops its own unique identity separate from the narcissistic parent, they begin to feel their power and control slipping away. Through whatever means necessary, the parent will insert themself into the dynamic, creating intentional chaos in order to reclaim their power and influence, even if it means undermining the marriage while emotionally harming their own child (and grandchildren) in the process.

The narcissist will slowly begin to devalue you as well as the relationship in general. They may start to voice their dissatisfaction in your career choices, your parenting style, or your ability to be a worthy enough partner to their child. They may start planting seeds of a smear campaign against you to friends and family members, and even to their own child. They sow doubt in their child's mind about the stability of their marriage by manufacturing concerns, such as implying possible infidelity or raising unfounded worries about your treatment of the children or your mental health. Rather than make direct accusations, the narcissistic parent will drop subtle hints to their child, laying the groundwork for manufactured distrust, which the narcissist will continue to reinforce throughout the marriage. They may also position you as the primary obstacle to their relationship with their child. You may become the target of blame, emotional abuse, and a smear campaign within the extended family.

When navigating a relationship with a narcissistic in-law, it is critical for you and your partner to always present as a unified front, aligned in your boundaries, to combat the manipulative efforts of the narcissist. Since it is not uncommon for the narcissistic in-law to target the grandchildren (especially if they are unable to regain access and control over their own child), it is also important to have age-appropriate discussions with your children about boundaries with their grandparent and the importance of informing the parents of attempts to cross those boundaries.

If you and your partner do not consistently present in alignment, the chances for erosion of the family dynamic increase considerably. This typically occurs when your partner sees nothing wrong with their parent's behavior. They are either unable to recognize the manipulation and coercive control because they too are enmeshed in the long-standing abuse patterns, or they avoid challenging their parent and thus continue to enable the behaviors. Your partner may tell you, "That's just how my dad is; you know he doesn't mean anything by it," or "She only said that because she loves us and wants the best for us." When your partner is unable or unwilling to set boundaries with their own parent, the narcissist continues to insert themself in your dynamic as a couple.

While some narcissistic in-laws see separation or divorce as a desired outcome, this is not always the case. Instead, many will seek to destroy the couple's emotional connection without necessarily encouraging divorce, since the end of the marriage could reflect poorly on them in the eyes of family, friends, or their community. To protect their image, the narcissistic in-law focuses instead on undermining the bond while at the same time helping to maintain a facade of stability to the outside world. In doing so, they establish themself as their child's relentless "rescuer," which reinforces the narrative that they "knew all along" that you were not right for their child, and it solidifies them as an irreplaceable central figure in their child's life.

Use the following strategies within a partnership to navigate the narcissistic in-law's manipulation and abuse:

- See a couples therapist with your partner (without the narcissistic parent present).
- The child of the narcissistic parent seeks individual therapy.
- All communication between the narcissistic parent and the couple should be in writing.
- Copy your partner on all correspondence, and loop them in if they were initially excluded.
- Jointly establish boundaries with your partner before implementing them.
- Always keep open lines of communication with your partner.
- Evaluate and revise boundaries as a couple when needed.
- Limit the amount of information that is shared with the narcissistic parent. This may include blocking or restricting them on social media platforms.
- Have ongoing age-appropriate discussions with your children about the importance of boundaries with their grandparents.
- Limit in-person interactions as needed. This may include holidays and special occasions like anniversaries and birthdays.
- Set strict boundaries around communication. This can include not responding to texts or calls after a certain time, no longer allowing unannounced visits, or preventing the narcissistic person from making plans with the grandchildren without the parents' consent.

REFLECTION

Describe a situation you have experienced (or observed in someone else's life) where a narcissistic in-law caused major strain or disruption within a partnership.

____

____

____

What boundaries were hardest for you to maintain? Why?

____

____

____

What boundaries would have been effective to enforce in the situation you described? Why?

____

____

____

Narcissists as "Friends"

Narcissists are extremely limited in their capacity to engage in and maintain healthy and reciprocal friendships. Their connections to others are based on the degrees to which people can meet their needs and provide them with something that they crave (e.g., social status, sex, money, caretaking).

As with most relationships involving a narcissist, the initial stages of these friendships often feel fast-paced and intense. Your friend may engage in constant texting and check-ins, make excessive and frequent efforts to get together, share extremely personal stories early on, and offer extravagant gifts and over-the-top compliments. The narcissist will also mirror your specific likes, interests, vulnerabilities, and flaws, making it appear as if the two of you have much in common. As in intimate relationships, these behaviors create the illusion of a deep bond before any real trust and confidence has had time to develop organically, increasing your willingness to let your guard down.

Once a deep and secure connection appears to be established, the narcissist will gradually begin to isolate you from your existing support network. This may initially sound like "I know you're good friends with him from college, but there is something about him I don't trust. I would be careful what you tell him" or "I know you have plans with your family tonight, but I was able to get tickets to the concert you wanted to go to." As the relationship progresses, the narcissist becomes increasingly more demanding of your time while simultaneously feeding you false narratives that your existing family and friends do not have your best interest in mind—that they are the only one who genuinely cares about you. This social isolation is a precursor to the narcissist's insidious deconstruction of your sense of identity via gaslighting and other coercively controlling behaviors within the friendship dynamic.

When playing the role of friend, a narcissist will never want to see you succeed. Unless your successes benefit them directly, they will sabotage your efforts in subtle ways. For example, they may deliberately give you bad advice, refuse to acknowledge your achievements, or deliberately start arguments with you during significant or meaningful events (e.g., five minutes before you board your flight to Florida for a family vacation, they text you that you're a horrible friend for being away on their birthday).

It is quite common for a narcissistic friend to be extremely unsupportive, emotionally unavailable, and inaccessible when you need them most. Should you be in crisis or experiencing emotional distress, such as a breakup, medical illness, or job loss, a narcissistic friend will quickly minimize your feelings, gaslight you into believing your reactions are invalid or dramatic, or shift the conversation to their own problems. They will treat you as if your needs are too much and your concerns are a constant inconvenience. Engaging with a narcissistic friend can feel quite literally like they are taking up all the energy within the space of the relationship. They show little genuine concern for your daily life, often coming across as disinterested or irritated when you share what you're going through, and may quickly shift the focus by one-upping your experiences, potentially leaving you feeling small, irrelevant, or even foolish for thinking what mattered to you was important. Conversely, however, you must always be available to support them during *their* times of accomplishments or distress, appeasing their needs at the expense of your own. According to the narcissist's narrative, attending to your own needs would make you a selfish and insensitive friend.

Any shift toward independence outside the friendship may be perceived as a threat to the narcissist's control. This can include making plans with other people, going to work-related events, returning calls outside a timeframe deemed appropriate by the narcissist, or even taking time to be alone. If the narcissist feels their control and influence slipping away, they will engage in manipulative tactics to regain their hold over the dynamic. This may present as starting arguments to disrupt your emotional state, feigning sickness or emergency as a way of getting you to attend to their needs immediately, or using guilt, shame, or silent treatments to make you believe you did something wrong—all of which continues to trap you within the abusive friendship. Attempts to end the friendship are frequently met with intensified love bombing and apologies, verbal abuse, threats to reveal your private information, or implementation of a smear campaign.

Narcissistic friendships can have a profound impact on you, draining you emotionally, physically, and even financially. Beyond the psychological, emotional, and relational damage of these friendships, they are extremely isolating and can take a toll on both your social and professional growth in life. The healthiest, most effective response within these types of friendships is to cut ties, seek out alternative social support, and disengage despite their continued efforts to provoke a response.

Use the following strategies to navigate the manipulation and abuse within a narcissistic friendship, during the process of disengaging, and in the aftermath of the relationship:

- Reconnect with social support.
- Lean on safe friendships.
- Celebrate your successes and achievements with supportive friends.
- Limit personal sharing of information.
- Set clear and consistent boundaries.
- Use a neutral tone and avoid emotion-based responses.
- Keep explanations minimal and avoid long justifications.
- Manage expectations of what they are able to offer you as far as support and empathy.
- Decline guilt trips by firmly saying no when pressured into plans or favors.
- If going no contact is not an option, go "low contact" by reducing contact gradually. (See chapter 7 for more on this.)
- Expect pushback in the form of love-bombing behaviors, guilt trips, and smear campaigns. Do not engage.

REFLECTION

Describe a situation you have experienced (or observed in someone else's life) regarding a friendship with a narcissist. Describe the specific ways the manipulation and abusive behavior showed up.

___

___

___

What boundaries were hardest for you to maintain? Why?

___

___

___

What boundaries would have been effective to enforce in the situation you described? Why?

___

___

___

Authority Figures

We've explored how to identify and navigate narcissistic abuse within our families, intimate relationships, and friendships. But what happens when the narcissistic relationship exists in your wider community? How do you manage these dynamics when the narcissist is your boss, religious leader, mentor, coach, or even favorite social media influencer? How can you recognize and respond to these relationships? And why do narcissists so frequently occupy positions of power?

Obviously, not all leaders and CEOs are narcissists. However, these roles do tend to attract individuals with higher levels of narcissistic traits than the general population—traits such as extreme confidence, grandiosity, self-focus, and persuasiveness. These characteristics can provide a distinct advantage in competitive executive and leadership roles, even though a leader's effectiveness tends to decline as narcissistic characteristics become more pronounced.

While most leaders will not meet the diagnostic criteria for NPD, the combination of narcissistic characteristics and organizational authority can create an unhealthy environment of control, manipulation, and power. This is particularly true in today's culture, where all too often, confidence is confused with competence and bold behavior is rewarded without sufficient accountability. Even when true competence, effectiveness, and strong leadership skills are absent, those who present with the image of dominance and bold confidence are often favored over those who possess more experience with quiet confidence.

Another reason those with narcissistic characteristics are more frequently placed in positions of power is because our society—particularly within social media and politics—normalizes and rewards competitive behavior over collaboration, and personal achievement over group goals, making it easier for a narcissist to rise in the ranks. This is especially true when their audience, whether company employees, hospital staff, or a religious congregation, is desperately searching for strong leadership during times of need and crisis.

As with all other narcissistic relationships, narcissists in positions of power and authority view independent thinking, values, and ideals as direct threats to their control. This is why narcissistic leaders reward blind loyalty. Rather than being helpful and supportive, they are dismissive, sabotage your efforts, or retaliate as you become increasingly autonomous—even if your ideas are extremely beneficial. (In this instance, the narcissist may punish you for your creative thinking while simultaneously taking full credit for your ideas.) Because the narcissist has instilled in their followers a tremendous sense of fear and self-doubt, people become extremely hesitant to voice their concerns, believing that it is safer to stay quiet. This is how a narcissist cultivates dependency within the group: by manipulating their followers' access to approval, opportunity, and safety. Over time, people learn to associate unquestioned compliance with the illusion of success and safety, often at the expense of their own career goals and aspirations.

Business Leaders

A narcissist in a professional leadership role can foster strong dependency among employees by limiting decision-making, selectively rewarding loyalty, and punishing those who offer independent ideas or challenge the status quo. Within this company's dynamic, you will eventually come to believe that your job security, growth, productivity, and professional worth is directly tied to your commitment and alignment with the narcissist. This carefully and deliberately crafted dependency continues to reinforce the narcissist's need for admiration, validation, and power.

Use the following strategies to navigate your relationship with a narcissistic boss, CEO, or executive:

- All conversations should be in writing. This is extremely important to protect yourself from gaslighting and to maintain clarity, particularly during times of heightened stress and emotions.
- Refrain from oversharing within the workplace. Only share with those you consider trustworthy.

- Document meeting notes, verbal agreements, and the details of any other relative interactions and events.
- Remain neutral and professional in your tone, word choice, expressed emotion, and body language.
- Seek out external support rather than relying on one person's feedback, approval, and opinions.
- Determine the actual power structure of the company. What is the organization chart of the company? Is there anyone who holds more power than the narcissist?
- Have an exit strategy (e.g., savings, outside references, timeline). Even if you choose not to follow through with your plan, sometimes just having the option offers a sense of choice and empowerment.

Spiritual Leaders

Narcissistic spiritual and religious leaders often use their authority and reach to control and manipulate their congregants, positioning themselves as the final authority on what is right or wrong in the eyes of their higher power. These toxic leaders create an intense dependency within their congregants, rewarding unquestioned obedience while shaming, isolating, and punishing anyone who dares to question their teachings and actions. It is common for narcissists in these positions to exploit religious beliefs to justify their own self-serving actions. They may instill the belief in you that your worth, right to belong, or salvation is solely contingent on the leader's approval. Over time, this toxic dynamic erodes your personal agency and instills high levels of fear and doubt, while keeping you and other followers psychologically (and often financially) tethered to the abusive dynamic.

Use the following strategies to navigate your relationship with a narcissistic religious or spiritual leader:

- Seek outside perspectives and assistance (i.e., those not connected to the leader).
- Discuss your religious beliefs with those outside your faith to gain alternative interpretations.
- Pay close attention to the group dynamics of the congregation. Are people manipulated by fear and shame? Is the leader idealized by the congregation despite their behavior?

Recognizing Narcissistic Leaders

Recognize possible red flags when dealing with narcissists in the community. Ask yourself:

- Do you feel wary of speaking your mind or making independent decisions?
- What are the personal and professional consequences for disagreeing or thinking freely?
- Do you have concrete knowledge of expectations and performance goals, or is this a constantly moving target?

Remember, when a narcissist is placed within a position of power, the manipulation and abuse is amplified. You are *not* overreacting. As you establish boundaries, be aware of the potential for backlash. Setting boundaries allows you to gradually take your power back from the narcissist. To regain their control, the narcissist may push back on your boundaries in the hopes that you will resort back to the status quo. This does *not* mean your boundaries are wrong—stay strong! Lastly, remember that leaving a job or a spiritual affiliation—or any relationship with a narcissist—is *not* failure: It is self-protection. Your safety and well-being matter more than being understood, especially when someone is committed to misunderstanding you.

REFLECTION

Describe a situation you have experienced (or observed in someone else's life) regarding a relationship with a narcissistic figure in the community. Describe the specific ways the manipulation and abusive behavior showed up.

How did you navigate this relationship? What was the outcome?

What boundaries were hardest for you to maintain? Why?

What boundaries would have been effective to enforce in the situation you described? Why?

Conclusion

Narcissists can show up in any type of relationship—you may have a narcissist as a family member, friend, romantic partner, supervisor, or community member. While the roles may differ, the behavior patterns do not. The narcissist's tactics may shift based on the relationship, but the function remains the same: to obtain power, control, and dominance over others. The way you navigate these dynamics remains the same as well: Prioritize your boundaries despite the discomfort, limit your engagement, surround yourself with trusted and supportive people, and give yourself grace rather than self-blame.

If you have experienced abuse at the hands of a narcissist, you are *not alone*, it is *not your fault,* and it does *not* mean there is anything wrong with you. You did nothing to deserve this, nor did you ask for this. The narcissist's behavior was, is, and always will be solely about them, *not* your worth.

6

An ACT Approach to Narcissistic Abuse

At this point, you have a stronger understanding of the narcissist's true intentions within the relationship, the playbook they follow, and the tactics they use. But how does this help you take back your power and rebuild your self-identity?

A central part of navigating a narcissistic relationship is recognizing that the narcissist's behavior is not yours to control, manage, or fix—nor is it your fault. Your power lies in how you choose to respond to it.

This chapter will offer uniquely effective strategies for navigating narcissistic abuse based on principles from ACT and mindfulness, paired with reflections and exercises that reinforce those principles. These strategies will continue the work you have already done in the previous chapters, allowing you to form highly efficient responses to abuse and coercive control, set and maintain effective boundaries, and develop your tolerance of the internal discomfort that arises in these dynamics, even after the relationship has ended.

Why ACT Helps Survivors Heal from Abuse

Most therapeutic approaches focus on analyzing your perception, challenging beliefs, or changing your inner experience to shift the dynamic in the relationship. But when it comes to narcissistic abuse, resolving your internal emotions and challenging your thoughts are not prerequisites for initiating change. What you need is to move forward alongside the pain, not wait for it to get better. By using ACT and mindfulness-based practices, you will learn to take the action available to you *today* that moves you closer to the life you value (and deserve), even if you feel afraid and uncertain.

As you've learned, the main ACT principles place emphasis on the following:

- Willingness to experience thoughts and emotions without trying to avoid, suppress, or control them
- Grounding yourself in the present moment
- Identifying your core values as your anchor points
- Aligning actions with values even when it may be uncomfortable

Through the use of ACT, I have witnessed incredible transformation in survivors of narcissistic abuse. I have seen them not only detangle themselves from the web of narcissistic abuse but also go on to form healthy relationships and lead extremely fulfilled lives. Moreover, the use of ACT strategies and mindfulness-based techniques significantly reduces the degree to which the trauma of the abuse interferes with their daily functioning and interpersonal relationships. In short, an ACT approach doesn't just help people navigate and escape abusive relationships; it helps them thrive.

One of the great strengths of ACT and mindfulness-based practices is that they teach us how to remain present, even in the face of emotional and cognitive discomfort. But it's important to understand that acceptance (the *A* in ACT) does not mean allowing, resigning, or excusing the abuse, control, and manipulative behaviors of narcissistic individuals. Rather, acceptance refers to your ability to notice thoughts, emotions, and bodily sensations as they arise without trying to suppress, avoid, or fight them—while still moving forward in ways that reflect your values. In other words, you are learning to make space for the uncomfortable thoughts and feelings triggered by the narcissistic abuse, not to accept or excuse the abuse itself.

For example, you might feel intense fear and self-doubt as you prepare to leave your job because of your narcissistic boss. ACT teaches you to notice these fears and use a variety of techniques to learn how to sit with your discomfort for what it *is*, not what it's *telling* you. Many people in narcissistic relationships become immobilized by such feelings—they know they want to (and probably should) leave their job, but they believe they cannot take action on that goal until they've overcome the fear and self-doubt they feel. ACT encourages you not to wait for those feelings and thoughts to go away, but to acknowledge their presence and tolerate the discomfort they cause while still taking the steps necessary to move toward what you value.

ACT also teaches you to not label or judge your painful emotions and intrusive thoughts as "bad" but rather to simply notice their occurrence. While other approaches may encourage you to analyze, search for meaning or a root cause, or persuade yourself out of feeling your pain, ACT teaches you to look at your pain with compassion and clarity as an active observer rather than push it away. Creating that space between you and your thoughts is what allows you to form your own self-narrative, which in turn helps you identify the personal values that will guide your healing journey. Again, this shift is critical for survivors, because narcissistic abuse conditions you to constantly second-guess yourself, suppress your needs, and seek the approval of the narcissist to stay safe. ACT interrupts that cycle by helping you reconnect to what truly matters to you, such as your safety, identity, and purpose in life.

Before we dive into the strategies for responding efficiently to narcissistic abuse, let's look at some common default responses to understand why an ACT approach is so effective in coping with narcissistic relationships.

Living in a State of Fight or Flight

The human body is well equipped to manage short-term stress and anxiety. It has a built-in mechanism known as your *fight-or-flight response*, which releases stress hormones, such as cortisol, in the presence of danger. These hormones activate symptoms such as racing heart, muscle tension, shallow breathing, and perspiration, just to name a few. While these symptoms don't feel great and can be scary, they are naturally occurring responses that are extremely effective in keeping you safe. They prepare your body to react appropriately to danger (e.g., running away, fighting back, or sometimes momentarily freezing) depending on what the situation requires while also signaling to your brain that it's time for some quick decision-making.

However, the brain and body are not well equipped to deal with prolonged stress. When flight-or-fight responses persist, stress hormones remain elevated and dysregulated, leading to cognitive, emotional, and physical health difficulties. This may include an overall weakening of the immune system, making you increasingly susceptible to illness. Chronically elevated levels of stress hormones such as cortisol can lead to inflammatory responses within the body, often resulting in conditions like irritable bowel symptoms, chronic pain, sleep difficulties, and joint pain. We often see this type of prolonged stress response in those who experience childhood abuse throughout their developmental years or domestic violence within their intimate relationships.

Living in a chronic state of fight or flight cultivates a state of *hypervigilance*—that is, you constantly scan your environment for any indication of danger (whether real or perceived). In a narcissistic abusive relationship, this may look like closely monitoring the narcissist's every move, carefully monitoring their moods, and assessing their words for subtle shifts in tone that could signal the onset of abusive behavior. Over the course of the abusive relationship, this hypervigilance becomes your baseline state. Your brain and body are so focused on survival that any thoughtful reflection or processing of your own emotions feels confusing and unsafe. In other words, it feels too scary, dangerous, and painful to be present within your own internal experience.

Trouble being present certainly isn't limited to survivors of narcissistic abuse. In today's chronically busy, commercialized world, we are constantly challenged by countless distractions to being present. But for narcissistic abuse survivors, the challenge of staying in the present moment goes one step deeper. You aren't just distracted from your internal experience; your chronic fight-or-flight activation almost completely disconnects you from your thoughts, emotions, and bodily sensations. This disconnection makes it difficult for you to respond from a place of choice versus habit and survival, which is why ACT is so valuable for those healing from this form of abuse. ACT strategies create space between you and your internal experiences so you can notice your emotions and thoughts rather than being controlled by them. This allows you to be deliberate in your actions, ensuring you are acting in line with your values rather than in service of the narcissist's narrative.

Avoidance

A primary aim of ACT is to target emotional and behavioral avoidance. As discussed earlier, when we feel uncomfortable emotions, many of us do whatever we can to get rid of them (e.g., doom scrolling, binge-watching TV, socially isolating, having a drink, diving into work). And while these strategies can be useful in the short term, they can interfere with long-term healing. It is not necessary to spend every moment of your day contemplating your discomfort. Sometimes you just need to give your nervous system a well-deserved break! But ongoing avoidance of your internal discomfort often results in behaviors that are in opposition to your values and lead to severe dysfunction in your daily life. For example, say you are scheduled to present a new product launch at your weekly status meeting. However, the thought of presenting to the entire office paralyzes you with anxiety, so you call out sick and ask your coworker to present in your absence. While this isn't necessarily healthy behavior, it is unlikely to result in any significant ongoing impairment. If, however, you continue to miss these meetings because of your anxiety, it will impact your day-to-day life and put you at risk of losing your job.

A chronic unwillingness to tolerate emotional discomfort by engaging in unhealthy behaviors can have profound implications on your mental and physical well-being. For example, someone who has experienced years of abuse as a child may turn to self-harming behaviors, such as cutting or disordered eating, or self-medicate with drugs or alcohol—all of which provide brief pain relief and a temporary feeling of being in control, yet cause significant dysfunction. Over the long term, these avoidant behaviors place a person at considerable risk for developing physical and psychological disorders, such as high blood pressure, anxiety, substance abuse problems, major depression, panic disorder, chronic worry, C-PTSD, and even suicidality.

If you are in a narcissistic relationship, avoidance has likely moved from an occasional coping strategy into a pervasive and dysfunctional pattern of trying to anticipate and control the narcissist's behavior. It shapes your daily life, influencing how you think and act. Emotional and behavioral avoidance in this context can appear as constant people-pleasing to avoid the anxious uncertainty of angering your narcissistic partner. As a child, you may have suppressed your own needs, such as giving up hobbies, as a way to temporarily avoid the fear of disappointing a narcissistic parent and minimize the damage to your self-worth. You may obsess over the "what ifs" by mentally playing out every scenario to avoid punishment from your boss, as it replaces your fear and uncertainty with a false sense of control. All of these behaviors are avoidant attempts to reduce pain and fear created by the narcissist. And while they may feel protective, they keep your attention and focus on the narcissist rather than on your own well-being and personal values.

The thing is, avoidance is still a form of engagement. And when you engage with your discomfort by fighting, suppressing, or organizing your life around not feeling it, the louder it gets and the more entrenched in it you become. Instead of focusing on what you find meaningful and acting from a sense of value and purpose, your entire life begins to revolve around protecting yourself from pain. Over time, avoiding the pain begins to interfere with daily functioning, isolates you from your interpersonal relationships, and takes you further away from your values.

It is important to emphasize that none of this suggests a failure on your part. You do not engage in avoidance and its associated behaviors (e.g., people-pleasing, excessive worry, addiction, self-harm, isolation) because you are weak; it is a response to feeling a lack of emotional and physical safety. When you do not have social support, adequate coping skills, or a safe space to process the chaos surrounding you, it becomes incredibly difficult to not only make choices that could help you heal from the pain, but also to even identify what those healthy behaviors are.

This is exactly where ACT can be so impactful. It offers practical ways to begin untangling from the web of emotional and cognitive discomfort and guide you back toward a sense of agency and reconnection with your values, and ultimately, your core self.

Strategies for Becoming More Present-Focused

As mentioned earlier, the *A* in ACT stands for *acceptance*. The principle within this word is that you hold space for all your thoughts and feelings, even when they are uncomfortable and painful, while continuing to engage in actions that are in line with your values and well-being, rather than constantly struggling against the pain.

In other words, our primary goal shouldn't be to *feel* better, but to *do* better by engaging in behaviors that are values-driven, even in the face of fear, doubt, and anxiety. The more we take action that aligns with our authentic self and true values, the more fulfilling our lives will become.

For survivors of narcissistic abuse, a key part of healing is reclaiming a sense of agency, independence, and personal power. As you move away from patterns of responding that were shaped by the narcissist's manipulation and control, and return your attention to your own inner experience, you disrupt the pattern of psychological control and begin to reconnect with your own sense of agency. The more mindfully present you are, the easier it becomes to consciously and intentionally make behavioral choices based on your own values rather than being driven by the narcissist's unpredictable abusive behaviors.

Many people assume that a relaxing, uninterrupted, or peaceful environment is necessary to be present. In fact, one of the biggest benefits of this skill is that it can (and should) be used regardless of your current surroundings, which you may have little control over. Whether driving in your car, sitting in a business meeting, lying in your bed, or facing a narcissist's onslaught of verbal abuse, grounding yourself in the present moment helps you remain centered and respond with intention.

Even in a moment of chaos or conflict, being present-focused allows you to ask yourself questions like the following:

- "Does this behavior move me toward or away from my values?"
- "If it moves me away, what is this avoidant behavior costing me? How does this not align with my values?"
- "In this situation, if I were to engage in a values-driven behavior, does it put my safety at risk?"
- "Is it too scary for me at this moment? If so, can I break it down into smaller, more manageable steps?"

While answering these questions won't change the narcissist's behavior (nothing can), it does help you stay connected to your authentic self, limiting the influence the narcissist has over your thoughts and feelings, ultimately depriving them of the supply they crave. The psychological, cognitive, and behavioral shifts you make while being present don't have to be big or dramatic to be impactful—all that matters is that they are intentional, reflect your values, and lead you toward a fulfilled and meaningful life.

Imagine on your birthday, your narcissistic ex sends you a letter from their attorney stating that they want an increase in custody from your existing 50/50 split. Unexpectedly faced with this letter on a day that is meaningful to you, you might feel a surge of anger, anxiety, and even panic.

You may feel compelled to interrupt your birthday dinner to immediately contact your attorney or ignore your dinner guests in favor of sending an outraged or panicked response to your ex. This is exactly what the narcissist's hoovering behavior is intended to accomplish. Why, at *this* moment, did your ex engage in *this* specific behavior? A narcissist wouldn't send that letter because they genuinely want additional custody of their children; they would send it to disrupt your enjoyment of your special day by targeting what makes you most vulnerable—your children—and ensuring that they still have access to your thoughts, emotions, and behaviors.

How might practicing staying present-focused help in this situation? It would mean pausing to observe your feelings and thoughts in the moment before acting. Rather than seeking immediate yet temporary relief from your panic and anger by rushing to contact your ex, this pause gives you space to feel your feelings rather than immediately acting on them. It also creates the clarity needed to choose a response that is values-driven. This could look like putting your email alerts on "do not disturb" with the intention of handling it the next day, turning off your phone, or briefly confiding the situation to a friend or loved one who is aware of your ex's controlling behaviors and can reassure you that sending you a legal custody letter on your birthday is, yet again, part of your ex's pattern of abuse and control. This can help you remain focused on being celebrated by all the people who love and support you.

Let's be clear: No one likes to experience emotional discomfort. But avoiding it only gives it more power to shape your reactions, relationships, and decisions. By being present with your pain, you strengthen your ability to act in ways that reflect your values and create a life that feels meaningful.

The following mindfulness and ACT-based strategies will help you become more familiar with how to create space between you and the narcissist's manipulation, control, and chaos. Regular practice will develop skills that help you rebuild your true sense of self and act in alignment with your values, even in the face of narcissistic abuse.

Being Present with Your Body

When you feel trapped in a narcissistic relationship dynamic, your brain can get caught in a loop of self-criticism, doubt, worry, or rumination of past interactions. When the brain is busy in this loop, it is extremely easy to disconnect from your body and what it is trying to tell you in the moment. Paying close attention to how your body physically feels is key to present-moment awareness. Noticing and honoring your basic physical needs—rest when you're tired, food when you're hungry, movement or breathing when you're anxious or frustrated—lays the foundation for reclaiming the autonomy and agency you deserve.

Because living with a narcissist often traps you inside your own mind with overwhelming thoughts and feelings of fear, shame, and doubt, you are likely rarely in tune with how your body feels. A mindfulness-based body scan offers a safe and effective way to shift your attention out of your mind and into the present moment by turning your focus to the physical sensations in your body.

When feelings of worry, outrage, or confusion make you feel paralyzed, a body scan helps you redirect your energy and attention to the existing moment with different cues, such as where in your body you feel tension or how your feet feel against the floor. It is a skill that gives you the chance to pause, release tension, and create space to notice unhelpful thoughts and feelings as passing experiences rather than becoming entangled in them and believing they define you. This perspective gives you the clarity to respond with intention and psychological freedom rather than reaction, gradually helping you reclaim your sense of self and autonomy.

EXERCISE: Toes to Nose

The following exercise is a quick and easy way to bring direct, focused awareness to each part of your body, helping you identify where you hold tension and giving you tools to consciously and intentionally release it. The squeeze and release action activates your body's relaxation response, which alerts your nervous system that you are safe and that in this moment, your fight-or-flight switch can be shut off. This gradually reduces cortisol levels, slows your heart rate, regulates your breathing, and helps you feel more present, relaxed, and clear-headed.

In a quiet space with limited interruptions, get into a comfortable position. You might sit on a couch or lie down on your bed or floor. Be sure to uncross your arms and legs.

First, direct your awareness to your toes. Flex your toes and hold for five seconds before slowly releasing over another count of five. As you engage in this exercise, notice the tension as you flex and release.

Repeat these directions for each of the following areas of the body, paying close attention to how each area feels as you hold and release.

- Feet
- Ankles
- Calves
- Knees
- Thighs
- Buttocks
- Pelvic area
- Stomach
- Fingers
- Wrists
- Hands
- Arms (lower and upper)
- Neck
- Jaw
- Nose

If your mind wanders at any point, that is okay (and expected)! Just bring yourself back to the moment by using your breath as an anchor point.

Do you notice a difference in how you feel before and after completing the body scan? Explain.

Which body part, if any, felt most tense?

Was there a part that was tenser than you had expected?

Was it difficult for you to remain grounded in the moment? What helped you return your awareness to your body?

Overall, would you say this experience was uncomfortable for you? Explain.

EXERCISE: Tracking Your Sensations

The intermittent nature of narcissistic abuse creates an environment filled with constant uncertainty and fears of danger even when there is no immediate threat present. You never know what to expect or which version of the narcissist you will encounter, leaving you in a chronic state of hypervigilance. The early recognition of stress in the body can alert you to take preventive measures before symptoms begin to escalate. Being present with your body can also help you differentiate between real and perceived threats of danger in the moment. In an environment where you feel powerless, being grounded in the awareness of your own body can create a sense of stability and empowerment.

Over the next couple of days, try being actively aware of how your body feels. Check in with yourself a few times a day, paying close attention to where you carry your tension. Using the tracking form that follows, record the body part(s) where you feel stress, along with a description of your immediate surroundings and your thoughts and feelings at that moment. (If you are having difficulty, refer to the previous *Toes to Nose* exercise to help you pinpoint the areas that require attention.) The more specific you can be in your description, the easier it will be to notice patterns in what triggers your stress and where it manifests in your body. Learning to recognize patterns like this can be a powerful tool for taking back ownership of your sense of self. They help reveal what in your life is contributing to distress and what is supporting your well-being, guiding you toward choices and behaviors that support your healing.

Sensation Tracking Form

Date and Time	Where Do You Feel Tension?	Where Are You?	Who Are You With?	What Are You Doing?	What Are You Thinking?

After completing your tracking form, use it to answer the following self-reflection questions.

Where did you tend to carry your stress and tension?

____

Is this what you expected?

____

Did you notice more stress in your body than you originally anticipated?

____

Did you notice a pattern in the areas where you hold your tension? Explain.

____

____

____

____

____

What variables did you notice contribute to your stress? (Consider who you were with, what you were thinking, and so on.) Do you recognize a pattern in the things that trigger your stress? Explain.

____

____

____

____

____

Are these patterns what you expected? ______________________

What are some behaviors you can change, add, and maintain to decrease your stress responses?

Change:

___

___

___

Add:

___

___

___

Maintain:

___

___

___

EXERCISE: Fishbowl Breathing

Believe it or not, most people breathe inefficiently. They engage in shallow breathing from their chest rather than their diaphragm. Shallow, rapid breathing is an instinctive response, driven by your fight-or-flight mechanism, for when you feel overwhelmed or anxious or when your brain perceives a threat of danger. It is meant to increase your oxygen availability quickly and prepare the body for immediate action; it is not meant for long-term regulation. Given the deliberately inconsistent structure of narcissistic abuse, your instinctive response of shallow breathing is a long-standing behavioral pattern triggered by perceived threats (e.g., someone's sudden shift in mood) rather than immediate physical danger. The overuse of shallow breathing in response to these perceived threats further exacerbates the fight-or-flight response, creating a vicious cycle.

It is important to note that shallow breathing isn't a personal flaw or mistake. It is a survival response designed to prepare the body to act in response to immediate danger. The problem arises when this response is triggered too often or for too long.

While this style of shallow breathing does have short-term benefits, proper diaphragmatic breathing is more effective and efficient. When you take a deep breath from your diaphragm, your abdomen should appear to gently expand as it fills with air. As you exhale, your belly naturally deflates, like a balloon losing air. This type of breathing allows you to take deeper breaths that draw in more oxygen. The more oxygen you bring into your body, the more regulated your body becomes, reducing stress hormones and providing a quick and easy way to regulate the nervous system. Proper diaphragmatic breathing has numerous benefits, including anxiety reduction, a reduction in panic symptoms, improvement in concentration and focus, and even improved sleep. This makes it a great anchor point when grounding yourself in the present moment. While the use of diaphragmatic breathing is an important life skill for anyone, it is particularly essential for those experiencing narcissistic abuse.

By training yourself in this efficient breathing technique, you can gradually shift your nervous system toward a calmer state, sending signals of safety to your brain and reducing the body's overactive threat response. Instead of being trapped in automatic fear-driven reactions, diaphragmatic breathing creates a momentary pause, giving you the opportunity to choose a response from a place of clarity rather than fear and doubt. As simple as it sounds, learning to breathe this way is incredibly empowering—with each step you take to improve your self-regulation abilities, the further you get from the controlling grip of the narcissist.

Your ability to self-regulate belongs to *you*; it is a skill the narcissist cannot access, manipulate, or take away from you.

This exercise will guide you through the steps to proper breathing and show you how to recognize the difference between chest breathing and diaphragmatic breathing. You'll learn how to catch yourself when you're breathing shallowly and how to correct it in the moment.

Stand in front of a mirror, placing one hand on your chest and the other on your belly. Take a regular shallow breath in, then exhale out.

Which body part moved? ______________________________

Keeping one hand on your chest and the other on your belly, close your eyes and picture a fishbowl in your belly. Take a deep inhale for five seconds, and as you breathe in, I want you to imagine filling up the fishbowl in your belly with water. Hold the breath for three seconds and then exhale through a count of five while imagining you are breathing out any excess water that spilled over the side of the fishbowl.

Which body part moved? ______________________________

Repeat the first two steps again, first with shallow breathing and then again with diaphragmatic breathing.

Do the two breathing styles feel different while practicing them?

____

____

Do you notice a difference in how your body feels after taking each type of breath?

____

____

____

EXERCISE: Being Present on Purpose

We rarely pay attention to how often we shift away from the present moment. This exercise demonstrates just how easily the mind wanders and how uncomfortable it can feel to simply be present. Strengthening this skill builds awareness of both your internal and external experiences and is another tool you can independently use to create space between you and the cycle of narcissistic abuse. It is within this space that you can learn to respond with intention rather than react from fear and emotional chaos.

Over a 30-second period, how long do you think you could stay present?

Record your estimate here: ______________________________

Now follow these steps:

- Find a space with limited interruptions.
- Get in a comfortable position.
- Set a timer for 30 seconds.
- Direct your focus toward one or more of the following prompts for the full 30 seconds. Whenever you notice that your thoughts have shifted away from the present moment, gently redirect them back to the prompt you are using.
    - Your breath
    - An object in your immediate surroundings that you can see
    - Something that you can hold, feel, or touch
    - A smell present in the room
- Repeat this process as many times as you need.

Keep in mind, the goal of this exercise is not necessarily to *stay* present, but rather to practice bringing yourself back to the moment when you realize your thoughts have drifted off.

Was your estimate consistent with your experience? ____________________

If not, why? ____

____

What do you find most difficult about being present?

____

____

What anchors were most helpful in bringing you back to center?

____

____

Was there a theme in the content of your distracting thoughts or emotions? What is the theme?

____

____

How do you see yourself making use of this skill set within your relationship?

____

____

In general, how will being more present impact your daily life?

____

____

Applying Cognitive Defusion

Cognitive defusion is another core process of ACT that helps you step outside your mind and become an observer of your thoughts and feelings rather than becoming enmeshed with them. Again, this is done by creating space between you and your internal experiences by simply noticing whatever comes up for you in the moment. Remember, from an ACT perspective, any thought or self-belief is an observable internal experience, not a hard truth.

Notice that cognitive defusion says nothing about trying to get rid of, challenge, or change unwanted thoughts. That's because trying *not* to think about a thought only makes it more powerful and pervasive. By attempting to silence, change, or argue away a thought, you end up making it your sole focus.

We all carry both helpful and harmful thoughts and beliefs about ourselves, formed in childhood as well as in our adult relationships and experiences. Cognitive defusion is about allowing these beliefs to arise, mindfully observing them without judgment, and allowing them to pass. Over time, this minimizes a belief's emotional impact and meaning while also reducing rigid thinking, worry, and rumination. With your mental energy freed from these exhausting thought loops, you can invest it into things that hold meaning, satisfaction, purpose, and value.

In a narcissistic relationship, especially, survivors' self-beliefs are not always internally derived. Instead, they are deliberately constructed by the narcissist over time through ongoing manipulation, gaslighting, and isolation. Applying cognitive defusion strategies within a narcissistic dynamic helps you create space between yourself and the false narratives you've been told. Over time, this separation reduces the narcissist's hold while offering you clarity into what beliefs reflect your true self.

Another important benefit of cognitive defusion is that it does not depend on the narcissist's behavior or intentions. You do not have to ask, hope, or wait for them to change to use this strategy. Just like the body scan and breathing exercises, this tool is entirely independent of the narcissist and their actions—you can apply it at any time without their awareness.

EXERCISE: Beach Banner

This exercise illustrates how separating yourself from an internal belief can influence how strongly you believe in it.

Start by identifying a deeply held belief you have about yourself that feels uncomfortable or maybe even painful. It could be something a narcissistic parent or spouse has repeatedly tried to convince you of, or maybe it is a belief you hold about yourself that has been reinforced by the narcissist in your relationship.

Repeat this belief three times to yourself, and afterward, take a minute to notice how you feel and what comes up for you.

Now imagine for a moment that you are at the beach. While sitting in your beach chair, you look up to the sky and see an airplane flying a banner across the ocean. Written on the banner is your belief. You watch the banner as it flies over the beach, reading the message until the plane is out of sight.

Comparing the two scenarios, did you notice a difference in how you felt internally? Did one feel less emotionally difficult?

____

____

____

Did you notice any shift in the way you perceive the belief? Explain.

____

____

____

This same strategy of defusion can also be applied to our unwanted, painful emotions. Many of us are taught from an early age that difficult emotions should be avoided—in other words, that it's bad to feel bad. Statements such as "Stop crying and grow up," "Don't worry so much," and "Just focus on the positive" send the message that we are at fault for our own internal discomfort and that we should avoid anything that has the potential to make us feel this way.

I am not suggesting you purposely go into situations that will make you feel bad or uncomfortable. What I am saying is that you should not avoid situations *just because* you want to avoid bad feelings. Avoiding situations to escape uncomfortable feelings often intensifies those feelings, especially when what you are avoiding is connected to something you deeply value.

ACT-based approaches suggest that instead of fighting to *not* feel or think about something uncomfortable, you need to allow yourself to have these experiences. By sitting with the embarrassment, hurt, or shame until it passes, your brain and body come to recognize that you *are* capable of sitting with your discomfort, that feelings are not scary, and most importantly, that they pass more quickly and easily when you do not struggle against them. The unbearable urgency of the feeling eventually passes, and your body lets it go.

When you struggle to get rid of difficult thoughts and feelings, you remain actively entangled with them, prolonging their impact. The solution? Drop the struggle. Instead of picking each thought and feeling apart to confirm or deny its validity, you can observe each one as if it were words on a computer screen. The words are separate from you, not part of you. This separation allows you to carry your thoughts differently by placing them outside your mind, freeing up your attention and time to focus on the things that truly matter to you.

Let's apply this now to the context of narcissistic abuse within a relationship. A common tactic used by narcissists is the exploitation of your emotions, particularly shame, guilt, and fear. Triggering these feelings within you makes it easier for the narcissist to control you. Desperate to eliminate these unwanted thoughts and feelings, you may engage in people-pleasing behavior, which suppresses your own needs and identity. You might neglect your own wants and needs, focusing solely on pleasing and proving your worth to the narcissist, even if it means sacrificing the things that are vitally important to you. By learning to separate yourself from these thoughts and feelings and simply let them exist rather than doing something to get rid of them, you decrease the power of the narcissist's psychological abuse and its influence over your self-identity and behavior choices.

EXERCISE: Unwanted Stuff

The purpose of this exercise is to take your internal discomfort, such as worry, self doubt, and uncomfortable thoughts, and place it outside of yourself by giving it observable characteristics and properties. Instead of being fused with your unwanted "stuff," you will become an active observer of it. This creates mental space that not only frees up your cognitive and emotional energy but also reduces the intensity, frequency, and impact of your discomfort. Your goal is to gradually become more proficient in separating yourself from the chaos in your mind and to become more tolerant of sitting with your unwanted stuff rather than desperately trying to avoid it.

Follow these steps:

- Find a comfortable seated position in a quiet room that will have limited interruptions.
- Close your eyes, and for a 60-second period, I just want you to worry—worry about everything that has been on your mind, everything that has consumed your energy for the last couple of weeks.
- Should your mind drift away, bring yourself back to your worry. Pay attention to the emotions that come up and how your body physically feels.

Afterward, take a moment to recall how you and your body felt during your 60 seconds of worry. Sit with those feelings for a moment while also paying close attention to any sensation in your body. As you sit with this, record your responses to the following questions.

If that uncomfortable feeling had a person's name, what would it be?

____

What shape would it take?

____

What color would it be?

____

What size would it be?

____

What would it smell like?

____

What noise would it make?

____

If you could touch it, what would it feel like?

How much would it weigh?

To the best of your ability, draw a picture of your unwanted stuff based on your descriptions.

Write a sentence as if you're talking about—or to—your unwanted stuff, using your descriptors. For example, "There's that Edward again, that foul-smelling tiny green triangle that won't stop buzzing in my ear."

Over the next few days, practice visualizing your drawing anytime you find yourself falling back into your "stuff." Talk to your unwanted stuff using the descriptive statements you provided. Pay close attention to how transforming your "stuff" into a picture creates distance between you and the thoughts themselves. Observing a picture that represents your "stuff" allows you to view it from an alternative perspective rather than being consumed by it. Notice the impact this shift in viewpoint has on your emotions, thoughts, and body.

Record your responses based on your experiences completing this exercise.

Do you notice a difference in how you experience your unwanted stuff when you objectify it versus keeping it internal?

What did you find most useful?

What, if any, part did you struggle with?

____

____

____

How do you see yourself utilizing this strategy within your narcissistic relationship?

____

____

____

EXERCISE: The Pink Pig*

This exercise demonstrates how in your effort to push away unwanted thoughts or emotions, you often end up making them more pronounced and powerful. The way to a peaceful mind isn't the absence of negative thoughts or moods, but rather your willingness to acknowledge and tolerate the discomfort of their existence.

Follow these steps:

- For 60 seconds, all I want you to do is think about a pink pig. Where is the pig? What does it look like? Pet it: What does it feel like? What is the pig doing?
- After 60 seconds, I want you to repeat the exercise, but this time, do *not* think about the pink pig. If you find yourself thinking about the pink pig during these 60 seconds, redirect your thoughts to something different. You may find that you need to remind yourself

* Adapted from Steven Hayes, PhD.

several times to not think about the pig. But whatever you do, do not think about the pink pig!

After you have completed both scenarios, reflect on the following prompts.

In which scenario did you think about the pink pig the most?

____

____

Which scenario felt most difficult? Why?

____

____

____

What conclusions can you draw from this exercise?

____

____

____

Think of a situation you recently experienced within your narcissistic relationship that resulted in a cycle of uncomfortable self-statements or unwanted thoughts. Rather than pushing away these thoughts, try using the Pink Pig approach. Record the self-statements and thoughts here.

____

____

____

____

What strategies did you initially use to get rid of the thoughts? Did they work? Why or why not?

After completing the Pink Pig exercise, what did you notice happened to the thoughts?

Shifting Your Language

Most of the time, your word selection happens automatically. You likely do not pause to consider how the phrasing of a thought shapes your emotional, cognitive, and behavioral responses. However, the words you use in your everyday conversations and within your own mind have a significant impact on how much you believe your thoughts and self-statements to be true. Even the slightest shift in language can profoundly alter how tightly you hold on to false narratives about yourself.

Adding a layer of separation between yourself and your thoughts by changing "I am" statements to "I'm having the thought that . . ." creates space to observe how your words influence your experience. For example, instead of saying, "I am too anxious to go out," you would say, "I'm *having the thought that* I am too anxious to go out." While this might seem like a minor shift, the impact is significant.

When you say, "I am too anxious to go out," you fuse yourself with your thought. It suggests that this statement *is* who you are at that moment, and your brain interprets this absolute statement as fact. On the other hand, when you say, "I'm having the thought that I am too anxious to go out," you are creating distance between yourself and the thought by taking an observer perspective. Our brains look at this as just words passing by and not as a solidified part of our identity. You very well may feel anxious, but you're less likely to have that thought influence your self-concept and decision-making. You can still go out *and* be anxious at the same time.

EXERCISE: Word Warrior

This exercise illustrates the ACT-based defusion technique of shifting the words we use in our everyday thoughts and conversations as a way of untangling ourselves from our negative self-statements and reducing the influence they have over our emotions and behavioral choices. Reframing your "I am" statements as "I am having the thought that . . ." can be an incredibly useful tool for challenging false narratives that have been instilled over time by the narcissist. By slowly dismantling the believability of this narrative, you can begin to reestablish your sense of self-identity and feel more empowered as you move closer to reconnecting with your own values.

Let's say your narcissistic spouse has kept you socially isolated for the last 20 years by convincing you that you're not intelligent enough to have meaningful conversations with people. You have accepted this as an absolute truth. As a result, you have very few friendships, and the ones you have are superficial. Reiterating to yourself "I am not intelligent enough" solidifies it as part of your identity. If, however, you repeatedly reframe this statement into "I am having the thought that I am not intelligent enough," it creates the distance necessary to challenge its validity and give you clarity on who is the original owner of that narrative.

The following is an example of a recurring thought many people experience in a narcissistic abusive relationship: "If I leave, no one else will want me."

Repeat this self-statement three times to yourself.

What are some feelings this statement triggers for you?

____

____

Now, repeat the following statement three times to yourself: "I'm having the thought that if I leave, no one else will want me."

What do you notice?

____

____

Repeat each statement again. Of the two statements, which one feels emotionally heavier?

____

____

Of the two statements, which one feels more like fact?

____

____

Now it's your turn. Think of a self-statement that you have been struggling with lately and record it here.

____

____

Rewrite this same statement with "I'm having the thought that . . ."

____

____

After repeating each statement, do you notice a shift in the emotional impact? If yes, how so?

____

____

Another simple word switch that is helpful when trying to separate yourself from your internal dialogue is replacing the word "but" with "and." For example, if I say, "I want to take a creative writing course, but I am anxious about sharing my work," I have automatically negated my initial intention of taking the course. In other words, I'm too anxious, so therefore I shouldn't take the course.

If, however, I say, "I want to take a creative writing course *and* I'm anxious," it suggests that both things can occur simultaneously. I can take the course and at the same time feel anxious. By replacing one simple word, you can promote values-driven behavior rather an engaging in actions fueled by emotions and false beliefs.

Try applying this idea to one of your own self-statements, first using the word "but" and then substituting it with "and."

____

____

How does the meaning change for you when the wording shifts?

____

____

EXERCISE: On Repeat

It's natural for our brains to attach emotions and meanings to words. But when these meaningful attachments work against us, it's important to learn how to separate the word from the meaning, or label, we gave it. This exercise creates separation through the simple act of repetition.

Have you ever noticed that a word starts to sound funny if you say it aloud multiple times in a row? It becomes more like a random sound than an actual word; it becomes disconnected from its meaning. Try saying the word "spider" aloud for 30 seconds and notice how it begins to sound strange, almost unrecognizable. The same thing can happen when you practice repetition with words that a narcissist weaponizes against you. For example, if a narcissist routinely calls you "worthless," it's easy for that word to work its way into your self-identity. But if you take control by intentionally repeating the word "worthless" aloud, outside of any context (that is, you're not calling yourself worthless; you're just repeating the word), it soon becomes just a meaningless sound. This helps you defuse from the abusive narrative forced upon you by the narcissist and recognize it as meaningless sound, not your truth.

Write one of your trigger words here:

____

What feelings and thoughts typically come up for you when hearing or reading this word?

____

____

Now, repeat your word for 30 seconds aloud.

What did you notice happened to the word?

____

____

Did your feelings and perception of the word shift the longer you repeated it? How so?

____

____

Try applying this strategy next time you find yourself triggered in the moment by a particular word or phrase the narcissist says to you. You can also set aside a few minutes per week to practice with specific words, so if they arise in conversation, their meaning and emotional impact have already been somewhat neutralized. Reducing the meaning and emotional impact of your trigger words takes away the narcissist's power and control over how you feel and think about yourself. It creates space to establish effective boundaries with intention and clarity, rather than reacting based on emotion, and allows you to reclaim your sense of self from the narcissist's narrative.

EXERCISE: It's All Just Nonsense

Another exercise that helps defuse an emotionally charged word is replacing it with made-up nonsense words. By intentionally substituting trigger words with absurd alternatives, you create distance from the emotional impact of the word, allowing you to untangle yourself from the meaning, feelings, and memories you've attached to the word. This disrupts the automatic emotional reaction the narcissist is trying to provoke from you and creates a pause that allows you to observe their manipulative patterns without being sucked back in. Your responses become more deliberate instead of emotionally reactive; you shift control away from the narcissist and reclaim your personal power.

As you work through this exercise, pay close attention to your thoughts and feelings. Become a mindful observer of whatever shows up without judgment or engagement. Simply allow yourself to experience everything in the moment while carefully noticing any shifts in your thoughts and emotions.

First, read the following message sent by Stephanie, a narcissist, to her ex-husband, Nick, about their daughter. Notice which words trigger an emotional response and pay close attention to shifts in your internal discomfort.

Maxie came home with food stains all over her shirt last time. Do you think this time you can be an actual parent and keep your child clean? Do you even watch her when she's eating at your house? Knowing you, you probably don't. She could choke on her food, and you wouldn't even notice. She looks sloppy and messy all the time when she comes back after your weekend. You're probably too busy with your girlfriends to notice. Do you even care about the damage you're causing our daughter? You're completely useless as a father. All you care about is yourself.

Although there are only a few direct insults aimed at Nick, the ongoing theme of accusations and blame make this message a clear example of verbal and emotional abuse. The message would almost certainly be emotionally triggering to Nick. However, it's what he decides to *do* with these overwhelming feelings that matters most. He could try to immediately get rid of these bad feelings (e.g., apologizing despite not doing anything wrong, arguing back, canceling plans with his girlfriend because he's too overwhelmed). However, these behaviors would be inconsistent with Nick's values and would give Stephanie exactly what she wants: to have power and control over his decisions, behaviors, emotions, and thoughts—especially how he sees himself as a father.

Now, let's read the same conversation again, but this time replace every "you" with a nonsense word of your choosing.

Maxie came home with food stains all over her shirt last time. Do ____________ think this time ____________ can be an actual parent and keep ____________'s child clean? Do ____________ even watch her when she's eating at ____________'s house? Knowing ____________, ____________ probably don't. She could choke on her food, and ____________ wouldn't even notice. She looks sloppy and messy all the time when she comes back after ____________'s weekend. ____________ is probably too busy with ____________'s girlfriends to notice. Do ____________ even care about the damage ____________ is causing our daughter? ____________ is completely useless as a father. All ____________ care about is ____________.

Now, refer to a conversation or a text communication you've had with a narcissist in your life. Using the word replacement technique above, go through your conversation and replace your trigger words with a nonsense word. You can also use a real word that does not fit within the context, such as "turquoise" or "roasted chicken."

Did you notice any change in your emotional response when reading the message with your nonsense word included? What kind of change did you notice?

____

____

Which version produced less internal discomfort while reading it?

____

What impact did this have on your overall perception of the meaning behind the message?

____

____

____

____

Valuing Your Values

As mentioned throughout the book, an important concept in ACT is identifying your values. Identifying what you truly value in life empowers you to ensure your actions are consistent with these values. This is essential to living a healthy, fulfilled life. The more your behaviors take you in the opposite direction of your values, the more unfulfilled you feel, placing you at a higher risk for developing stress, anxiety, depression, and even physical health issues.

Goals Versus Values

You might be wondering about the difference between goals and values. Think of your values as a large umbrella, while your goals are the people standing underneath. A goal is an outcome that is specific, repeatable, and measurable. For example, if you value being a present and involved parent, a goal might be to turn your phone off every evening at 6 p.m. so you can spend quality time with your child.

Measuring this goal is straightforward: Did you turn your phone off at 6 p.m. on Monday night? Yes or no? It involves a concrete action that is easy to measure and simple to repeat.

In today's busy, faced-paced world, it's easy to slip into autopilot. Most of us are rushing from one thing to the next, relying on habits and shortcuts to save time and reduce stress. When that happens, we're not always fully present or mindfully considering whether our behaviors line up with our values. This is not a failure. This occasional detachment from our values is a normal, human response to life's constant demands. But for someone who has experienced intense coercive control within a narcissistic abusive relationship, that disconnection is profound. Sometimes, if narcissistic abuse has gone on for years, you may not even realize how far away it has taken you from what truly matters to you.

Throughout your relationship with the narcissist, you may have learned to suppress your own needs, interests, and beliefs to "control" the narcissist's behavior toward you; if you act like the person they want you to be, they are less likely to be abusive toward you. But as you've likely learned firsthand, attempting to control a narcissist's emotions and behaviors only leaves you feeling more anxious, resentful, and defeated. It also keeps you trapped in a vicious cycle of false hope. The more you allow the illusion of control to influence your actions, the more out of control you will feel.

Therefore, the most important question is: "How do I immediately respond to the urge to relieve my discomfort?" If you act on the urge by adjusting your own responses in an (unsuccessful) effort to control the narcissist's behaviors, you'll wear yourself out emotionally and physically (and ultimately give the narcissist more control over you). If, however, you sit with the urge, it *will* pass, and you will have conserved your emotional, cognitive, and behavioral energy. By simply holding space for the uncomfortable feelings the narcissist triggers for you, without acting on those feelings, you create room to choose a response that intentionally targets their behavior's function and is values-driven rather than emotion-driven.

It's worth noting that behaviors that make you *think* you're regaining control (e.g., worry, anticipating their needs, people-pleasing) may feel safer in the moment, while behaviors that result in a true sense of control are usually the behaviors that initially feel the most uncomfortable. Moreover, breaking away from the manufactured values the narcissist instilled in you can be a scary and confusing process. Don't let the challenge and fear of this inner work deter you—understanding what you truly value in life is an integral part of reclaiming your identity and healing from narcissistic abuse. Uncovering your true values allows you to make decisions based on your core self rather than in the service of fear, guilt, or the narcissist's expectations of you. Your values become your internal GPS, guiding your choices, boundaries, and behaviors as you navigate life after breaking free from the narcissist's control.

EXERCISE: Egg-cellent Customer Service

This visualization exercise demonstrates how trying too hard to control something we have no control over ends up giving us more of what we don't want—further loss of control.

Imagine that you have been given the responsibility of delivering a very rare egg to a customer who lives down the street from your farm. You must carry the egg in your hand and personally deliver it to your customer. It is your job to protect the egg, ensuring it does not fall, crack, and break.

What is your immediate solution to safely deliver the egg to your customer?

The safest way to carry the egg would be to gently rest it in the palm of your hand and loosely cup it with your fingers. In other words, the less you squeeze (control) the egg, the safer it will be. Most people's knee-jerk solution would be to hold the egg tightly to protect it, but what happens if we hold a raw egg tightly in our hand? It cracks. And so, in your effort to control and protect the egg from cracking, you end up with the exact result you didn't want—a big mess. This same concept applies when attempting to control the behaviors and mood of a narcissist. The more time and effort you spend trying to change things out of your control, the more chaotic, frustrated, and out of control you feel.

Briefly reflect on how the concept of "controlling the uncontrollable" plays out within your own narcissistic relationship.

EXERCISE: Visualizing Your Values

Rediscovering your authentic values puts you on the path to reconnect with your true self. This acceptance-based exercise will help you identify your core values, set specific and measurable goals, and recognize obstacles that may arise, ensuring your behavior remains aligned with what matters most to *you*.

Record three of your core values:

1. ______________________________

2. ______________________________

3. ______________________________

For each value you listed, write three goals that align with that value. Remember to make each goal specific and measurable. Then identify at least one behavior you've seen in yourself that aligns with that value, and one behavior you've seen in yourself that takes you away from that value.

Example value: *I value living a healthy life.*

Goals that align with your value:

1. *Limit my social media use by not using these apps after 6 p.m.*
2. *Food prep for the week every Sunday night.*
3. *Take a 20-minute walk twice a week for a month.*

Behavior in line with example value:

I put my phone in a drawer during dinner so I couldn't look at it.

Behavior in opposition to example value:

I sometimes scroll on my phone while helping my daughter with her homework.

Value 1: ______________________________

Goals that align with your value:

1. ______________________________

2. ______________________________

3. ______________________________

Behavior in line with your value:

____

____

Behavior in opposition to your value:

____

____

Value 2: ____________________________________

Goals that align with your value:

1. ____________________________________
2. ____________________________________
3. ____________________________________

Behavior in line with your value:

____

____

Behavior in opposition to your value:

____

____

Value 3: ____________________________________

Goals that align with your value:

1. ____________________________________
2. ____________________________________
3. ____________________________________

Behavior in line with your value:

____

____

Behavior in opposition to your value:

____

____

What did you find most difficult about identifying your values?

____

____

Do you tend to spend more time engaged in behaviors that take you closer to your values or further away?

____

____

____

What are some reasons you may engage in behaviors that are inconsistent with your values?

____

____

____

What are some ways you can increase participation in values-driven actions while decreasing those that go against your values?

Narcissists thrive on instilling doubt, confusion, and fear in you as a way to maintain power and control. You become trapped in a vicious cycle of abuse while internalizing the narcissist's narrative as fact. The core skills of ACT discussed in this chapter—being present-focused, becoming an active observer of your internal experiences, tolerating discomfort rather than attempting to control or avoid it, and anchoring your actions in your values—help pull you out of that cycle. These strategies equip you with the tools to disentangle yourself from self-doubt and confusion and to weaken the power of the narcissist's coercive control tactics, opening the door for you to question the narrative you've been conditioned to believe. It is within this space that you become less consumed by the chaos and better able to recognize the patterns of the narcissist and identify the function of their behaviors.

These ACT strategies are more than just coping skills to help with symptom relief. They are life skills that move you toward empowerment and purpose, cultivating the mindset you need to resist the psychological chaos. In the next chapter, you'll learn how to navigate the safety risks, logistics, finances, legalities, and other practical barriers deliberately set in place by the narcissist to make leaving feel impossible. Together with your empowered mindset and newfound life skills, this guidance will help you to finally break free.

7

Escape

Ending a relationship with a narcissistic abuser is the rare type of breakup that requires an actual exit strategy. It can't be overlooked that escaping this type of relationship carries heightened risks and lasting psychological effects. As we discussed in chapter 2, escaping the narcissistic abuse cycle, regardless of relationship type, is not an easy task, nor does it mean the abuse has ended. Ending the relationship is uniquely confusing, frightening, and at times dangerous, often requiring multiple attempts to end the relationship for good. Even after the relationship itself has been terminated, psychological and emotional abuse frequently persists, continuing to impact you long after the physical separation has occurred.

The end of a relationship represents the ultimate loss of control and power for the narcissist. They will feel their grip slipping, their power weakening, and their supply diminishing. This loss is intolerable to them—and combined with their entitled sense of ownership over you, it fuels the ongoing abuse and coercive control that continues long after separation.

For that reason, ending this type of relationship is often a process rather than a single decisive moment. Navigating this process with a narcissist, regardless of whether the relationship is intimate, familial, or a friendship, is complex. However, because intimate relationships with narcissists carry a significantly higher risk of retaliation, stalking, and physical violence in the first few weeks of the separation, this section focuses specifically on escape strategies for intimate partnerships. While the underlying dynamics of control and manipulation are the hallmarks of all narcissistic relationships, the safety considerations involved in leaving an intimate relationship require a deliberate, structured, and protective game plan.

How to Devise an Exit Strategy

Many of my clients describe their relationships with a narcissist as chaotic, frightening, and paralyzing, yet the prospect of leaving often feels even more terrifying and immobilizing. Not only are you faced with the practical consequences of leaving—financial limitations, legal and custody issues, and limited social support—but it also brings the fear of what your future may hold, of having to rebuild your sense of who you are outside of the false narrative created by the abuser. No matter how firm you are on your commitment to escaping the situation, your brain can easily become overwhelmed with both the "what ifs" of your future and the practical realities of leaving. In times of uncertainty and fear like this, our brains instinctively seek predictability. Even coercively controlling patterns of behavior, if familiar, can continue to provide a false sense of predictability and comfort. This can make you increasingly more vulnerable to the narcissist's manipulation via post-separation abuse, including escalation of love-bombing efforts; psychological, emotional, and legal abuse; smear campaigns; threats of physical violence; intimidation; and stalking behaviors.

Amid this firestorm of post-separation abuse, a well-thought-out, tangible exit strategy helps reduce some of the uncertainty around leaving and redirects your attention onto concrete steps that focus on what matters most: getting out safely. It should go without saying that a safe, planful, and effective exit strategy can't be formulated on the spot or hastily decided the night before. Impulsive or opportunistic attempts to leave the relationship increase your vulnerability to coercive control and post-separation tactics, and elevate the risk of emotional manipulation, retaliation, and physical danger. A well-formulated exit strategy should be completed (as much as possible) in advance to maximize the likelihood of success. It must be feasible, concise, and focused on the immediate and practical necessities required to leave the relationship safely.

Secrecy

It is important that you do not inform the narcissist of your intentions to leave, for a couple of reasons. First, you, as a survivor, are at the highest risk of physical violence during the leaving process. If possible, it is best to tell the narcissist you are ending the relationship only *after* you are safely established with the necessary resources in place.

Second, it is highly likely that the narcissist will engage in numerous manipulative strategies to draw you back in. It is important that you anticipate these types of behaviors and do not engage. These control tactics are specifically designed to distract you from your goal of leaving and to manipulate you back into the abuse cycle.

Lastly, the narcissist will enlist their flying monkeys to get as much information as possible about your plans so they can sabotage your efforts. Therefore, it is essential to be very discerning in who you speak to about your plans to leave the relationship. There are going to be people in your support network who do not understand the complexities of narcissistic abuse, making them more likely to be swayed by the narcissist's narrative. If these people are aware of your decision to leave, they may attempt to intervene by convincing you to give the relationship another chance. For this reason, it is important to inform only those who will play a necessary role in your exit plan and who you are certain will not be influenced by the narcissist's manipulation. The more information you share about your plans to leave, and the more people you share it with, the greater the opportunity for the narcissist, as well as others, to undermine your efforts, increase your exposure to their manipulation, fuel self-doubt, and ultimately draw you back into the relationship, all during a period when you are already highly fearful and emotionally vulnerable.

Obtain Legal Counsel

When divorcing a narcissistic partner, nothing is more important to your safety and success than finding the right legal representation. I always advise my clients, particularly those who share children with a narcissistic partner, own businesses together, or have joint assets, to obtain legal counsel or, at the very least, consult with an attorney during their planning process before exiting the relationship. It is important that the person leaving is aware of their legal rights, such as possession of the home and parental rights. There are several online resources available that can direct you toward attorneys and advocates who are proficient in this domain.

Many attorneys will offer a free initial consultation for prospective clients. It is equally important that you ask the attorney questions about their previous experience with *high-conflict divorces* (as these situations are commonly referred to in the family court system) as well as custody disputes, narcissistic abuse, and domestic and intimate partner violence. In addition, it is beneficial to assess the attorney's level of familiarity with the various forms of coercive control, including legal and financial abuse.

When seeking legal representation, certain beliefs or recommendations should immediately raise concerns. One significant red flag is an attorney who frames a high-conflict divorce as the result of *both* parties being equally difficult. In cases involving narcissistic abuse, the conflict is not mutual. It is deliberately created by the abusive partner as a means of maintaining control and power. A "both-sides" perspective reflects a fundamental misunderstanding of coercive control and narcissistic abuse, and can inadvertently reinforce your internalized blame, suggesting that you are equally responsible for the abuse you have endured.

Another red flag is an attorney who is unaware of, or minimizes, the systemic flaws of the family court system, particularly its failure to adequately protect children from abusive parents. Family courts have historically separated abuse of a parent (most often the mother) from abuse of the child. If an abusive parent has not directly or physically harmed the child, they are frequently still deemed a "fit" parent, despite a clear pattern of coercive control, emotional abuse, and psychological harm directed at the other parent. An attorney who does not understand this distinction, or who fails to strategically account for it, may be ill-equipped to protect you or your children during the divorce process.

Any suggestion by your attorney that you engage in coparenting counseling with your narcissistic partner is also a red flag. Encouraging increased communication with an abuser demonstrates a lack of understanding of narcissistic abuse, as further contact can be retraumatizing and unsafe. The narcissist thrives on this forced collaboration, and survivors are often pressured within the family court system into these arrangements under the guise of cooperation or "doing what's best for the child."

Finally, a knowledgeable attorney must understand how allegations of a debunked legal strategy known as *parental alienation* are frequently weaponized by the abusive parent in custody disputes. The narcissist may claim that you are engaging in parental alienation—that is, deliberately isolating the child from them because you want to sabotage their relationship with the child—when in reality, if you are trying to limit your child's contact with their other parent, it is only to protect the child from ongoing emotional, psychological, physical, or sexual abuse. This legal term has repeatedly been debunked and rejected by both psychiatric and legal organizations, but it continues to be used strategically in court to shift blame, punish, and reassert control over survivors—especially women. An attorney who fails to recognize this legal tactic, or who minimizes these claims, may inadvertently facilitate the narcissistic parent's manipulation.

Choosing the right legal representation isn't just about skill level; it's about choosing a lawyer who makes you feel safe, validated, and protected. This doesn't mean you need an attorney who is an expert in narcissistic abuse and coercive control, but you do need one who listens and believes you when you describe what you've lived through, takes your concerns seriously, and is receptive to learning how manipulation and coercive control show up in the divorce process. They should be willing to incorporate this understanding into their legal strategy, particularly around custody issues. Understanding this form of abuse doesn't just support you, but it also gives your attorney a clear picture of the blueprint of narcissistic abuse, allowing them to better anticipate the narcissist's predictable legal tactics, counter their manipulative strategies, and avoid having the abuse reframed as mutual conflict. An attorney who minimizes or dismisses these dynamics can unintentionally place you and your children at greater risk for further abuse.

When you begin working with an attorney, it can be extremely helpful to explain the abuse dynamics you experienced and how coercive control shows up in the relationship. In some cases, you may initially find yourself in the position of teaching your attorney about narcissistic abuse. Most competent attorneys are open to learning, and providing context, documentation of behavior patterns, and information on narcissistic abuse from reputable resources can help them better understand the events that will undoubtedly arise during the divorce process. However, if your attorney is dismissive or consistently reframes the dynamic as a mutual conflict despite your best efforts to educate them, it is recommended that you seek different legal representation if possible. This is not a failure on your part to educate your attorney, but rather a smart and protective legal decision.

This is why the initial consultation process is so important. Consultations are not just about whether an attorney will take your case; they are an opportunity for you to assess whether they are familiar with coercive control tactics and custody-related manipulation, whether they are willing to understand these complex relationship dynamics, and whether you feel heard, believed, and safe with the person who will represent you. If you are unsure where to start, many of my clients have found qualified attorney referrals though trusted support networks, such as domestic violence organizations, peer support groups, communities of survivors, and mental health providers who specialize in narcissistic abuse.

Take Inventory of Your Finances

As you know, it is common for narcissists, whether family members, spouses, or business partners, to use finances as a tool of power and control. Financial abuse within these relationships typically involves limiting your knowledge of financial information and access to funds. When devising an exit strategy, it is critical to gain as much knowledge as possible about your financial situation. What financial institutions do you use, what types of accounts do you have, and do you have access to them? I recommend composing a master list of all account numbers, logins, passwords, and credit card information. This also includes a copy of your most recent tax return, mortgage and other loan statements, and any other financial or investment documents. I also recommend running a personal credit check early in the leaving process, because financial abuse by a narcissistic partner can seriously damage your credit without your knowledge. Unfortunately, it is all too common for the narcissistic partner to have secretly accrued massive debt over the course of the relationship and have loans, lines of credit, and credit card accounts in their spouse's name. Because of this, it is often helpful to consult with an accountant or financial advisor, if possible, to obtain guidance and insight into what your next steps should be.

Being aware of your financial standing is a crucial step in protecting yourself and planning a safe escape. It also helps you understand your financial options when preparing to leave the narcissist, such as whether you need to borrow money from someone in your support network (if it's even an option), open a separate bank account, lease a car, or determine how much you can realistically financially support yourself. This financial awareness allows you to be strategic in your planning and access necessary resources ahead of time.

Retain Personal Documents

If possible, find and retain official versions of your birth certificate, Social Security card, marriage license, passport, and other personal documents. When you need them in the future, it will not require you to depend on or have contact with your abusive partner.

When leaving a narcissistic partner, certain legal and financial documents are frequently weaponized as a means of maintaining control and power over you. The narcissist may refuse to hand them over, destroy them, or claim they are "lost," forcing you to navigate the lengthy and frustrating reapplication process on top of all the other stress, manipulation, and abuse you are experiencing. These documents are also essential to many of the critical steps in safely leaving, including opening a separate bank account, leasing or buying a home or car, or even something as simple as updating your home address. Without them, you face unnecessary obstacles that can delay your exit, increase vulnerability to the narcissist's manipulation, and pose an increased threat to your safety.

Pack a "Go Bag"

Have a bag packed and ready with a few changes of clothing, necessary toiletries, medications, important legal documents, cash or a prepaid credit card, and any personal electronics, such as a cell phone (or a prepaid cell phone if there is a risk of the narcissist shutting off your service), laptop, or tablet. It is best to keep your bag hidden but easily accessible. This could be in the trunk of your car, at your office, or at a trusted friend or family member's home.

Given the increased risk of physical violence during this time, leaving may require an immediate exit, particularly if you feel your safety is at risk. Having a bag prepped ahead of time gives you the flexibility to leave quickly, without having to frantically locate and pack your essential items, particularly during a time of heightened emotions within a potentially unsafe environment.

Enlist Social Support

It is likely that the narcissist has isolated you from those closest to you. Because of this, it can be extremely difficult and overwhelming to identify social support. You may feel a tremendous amount of guilt reaching out to loved ones that you have limited or cut off contact with during the relationship. Perhaps it isn't your first attempt at leaving and you feel a sense of shame and embarrassment reaching out for support yet again. Keep this in mind: Most people in your support network care about you and love you. It's likely they have been concerned for your well-being and are relieved that you are reaching out for help.

It is helpful to identify one or two people within your support network who are willing and able to help keep you physically safe, but just as importantly, they need to serve as a steady voice of logic, clarity, and reality during an especially confusing and emotionally vulnerable time. Ideally, they will be people you trust and feel safe with, and who understand your specific needs and concerns. Because gaslighting erodes your ability to trust your own perceptions, these people can help you regain clarity and confidence in your interpretation of situations, recognize the narcissist's manipulation, and resist engaging with them. By supporting you in not responding, they help protect you from the narcissist's inevitable attempts to pull you back in.

For Loved Ones of Survivors . . .

Distraught family members often ask how they can persuade their loved one to leave an abusive relationship with a narcissist. Although it's done with good intentions, repeatedly expressing concern and showing anger, annoyance, or disappointment can unfortunately have the adverse effect of driving your loved one away or making them hesitant to share information with you. The best approach is to offer unconditional love and support, assuring them that if, and when, they decide to leave the relationship, they can rely on you to guide them through the difficult and often scary process.

Secure a Place to Stay

One of the many reasons people remain stuck in a narcissistic abusive relationship is because they have nowhere else to go. The absence of a support network and limited financial resources can make finding a safe place incredibly difficult. This is why reconnecting with trusted family and friends before leaving is a crucial part of a well-planned exit strategy. A strong support system can help you gather the resources needed to create a secure environment. If reconnecting isn't an option, there are organizations and resources specifically designed to help people leaving abusive relationships to locate safe housing and support, especially if you are financially unable to secure housing or a temporary location (e.g., hotel, short-term rental).

Local domestic violence shelters and crisis centers often provide emergency housing, confidential safety planning, advocacy, and help navigating your next steps. The National Domestic Violence Hotline can connect you to shelters and services in your area without requiring you to disclose more than you're comfortable sharing. You can also text 211 or visit 211.org to be connected to local emergency housing, social services, and domestic violence resources. Community women's centers offer direct referral pathways to safe housing, legal, and financial support. If you are already working with a therapist or domestic violence advocate, or you take part in a therapeutic support group, they will be able to help you confidentially connect with necessary resources.

EXERCISE: Exit Strategy Checklist

- ❒ Contact an attorney: ______________________________
- ❒ Confide in one or two people about your exit plan and enlist their help: ______________________________
- ❒ Find a safe place to stay: ______________________________
- ❒ Gather all important documents:
    - Driver's license
    - Passport
    - Birth certificates and marriage license
    - Social Security card
    - Medical records
    - Financial documents (e.g., accounts, mortgages/loans, taxes)
    - Other: ______________________________
    - Other: ______________________________

- ❒ Make a master list of all login information, passwords, and user IDs:
    - Email
    - Social media accounts (even if you don't use them)
    - Banking
    - Bills
    - Patient portals
    - Other: ______________________________
- ❒ Set up a new email account and change *all* existing passwords and logins
- ❒ Temporarily take down social media accounts and/or block your ex and extended circles
- ❒ Purchase a prepaid credit card
- ❒ Purchase a prepaid cell phone
- ❒ Have some cash on you if possible
- ❒ List important phone numbers:
    - ______________________________
    - ______________________________
    - ______________________________
    - ______________________________
- ❒ Pack a to-go bag to be left in a safe place (e.g., the trunk of your car or with a trusted friend or family member):
    - Changes of clothing
    - Necessary toiletries (including menstrual products if needed)
    - Medications (including over-the-counters)
    - Important documents (ID, passport, etc.)
    - Prepaid credit card and/or cash
    - Laptop or tablet

REFLECTION

What else would you include on your checklist as part of your exit plan?

Are there any challenges, obstacles, or difficulties that might prevent you from creating a complete checklist?

Are there any challenges, obstacles, or difficulties that might prevent you from being able to formulate a *safe, well-developed* plan?

What are some potential solutions to the obstacles you previously named?

Preparing Yourself to Navigate Post-Separation Abuse

The abuse following separation can often be worse than the abuse endured during the relationship itself, including the heightened risk for physical violence. The narcissist is now working to bring you back into the abuse cycle and gain further supply. Similar patterns of behavior may show as the narcissist fights for control; they routinely target what they know you will fight most fiercely for, especially after the relationship has ended.

Your Children

Post-separation, narcissists often use their children as a tool of manipulation with the intention of seeking revenge, punishment, and establishing control over their ex-partners.

Within the family court system, it is common for a narcissistic parent to position themself as caring, cooperative, and the ultimate victim in the custody dispute. They often claim parental alienation, arguing that their relationship with their child is deliberately being sabotaged and obstructed by the other parent. But a narcissistic parent doesn't want custody of their child—they just want the power and control that comes from denying you custody. These accusations are a strategic attempt to discredit you by casting you as unstable, selfish, and unfit.

Your Money

Financial abuse throughout post-separation can take several forms. It can be the refusal to comply with court-ordered alimony or child support, or a prolonging of the legal process that forces the other party into financial hardship.

The narcissist may also cancel credit cards, close bank accounts without any notification, withdraw funds from joint accounts, sell off properties and assets without your knowledge, accrue debt in your name without your awareness, and change all login and password information.

While on the surface it may appear as though the aim is to completely deplete you of all available finances, money is just a vehicle. The true purpose of the narcissist's financial abuse is to instill a sense of fear, helplessness, and dependency in you. This increases the likelihood of forced contact for essentials like housing, transportation, legal costs, or basic living expenses, ultimately manipulating you back into their life.

Your Legal Rights

Legal abuse is a powerful control tactic resulting in ongoing coercion, abuse, and manipulation. In these situations, the narcissist weaponizes the legal process to intimidate, control, and punish you. They exploit legal loopholes, refuse to comply with court orders, file meritless motions, and misuse protective orders to prolong proceedings, drain your resources, and exhaust you (emotionally, financially, psychologically) until you eventually give in to their legal demands.

Your Character

A narcissist's character assassination serves two primary purposes. The first is to undermine the survivor's credibility so they are less likely to be believed. It's important to understand that the narcissist's smear campaign is rarely sudden. It is often already in motion long before the relationship ends.

The narcissist also uses character assassination to isolate the survivor from their support network, including family, friends, neighbors, and colleagues. By spreading lies, half-truths, and quiet accusations early in the relationship, they plant seeds of doubt that create a subtle wedge between the survivor and those they trust most. Over time, the narcissist deliberately reinforces this false narrative, widening the gap until they have completely isolated the survivor from their support network. With no one left to confide in or turn to for help, the survivor feels pressure to reconnect with the narcissist. The dependency, vulnerability, and isolation are by design and used to manipulate the survivor into believing they cannot cope without relying on the narcissist.

Your Psychological and Emotional Well-Being

Psychological and emotional abuse takes on a different form post-separation. Because the narcissist no longer has direct access to you, they may now use stalking behavior, intimidation, incessant verbal abuse and gaslighting via text messages, character assassination, threats to divulge personal information, or fear of physical harm. The narcissist may contact you unexpectedly on meaningful days, such as your birthday or the anniversary of a loved one's passing, or unleash a social media campaign showing off their newest relationship shortly after a breakup to promote their image of a loving partner.

Post-Separation Contact

While the ultimate goal post-separation is to go no contact with the abuser, this is not always possible. As mentioned in chapter 5, you may need to parent with them or see them in other scenarios. This requires you to set both internal and external boundaries, but the boundaries may also need to be fluid depending on the context. In other words, post-separation dynamics with the narcissist may shift over time.

In these cases, a variation of no contact referred to as *low contact* can be used. Low contact means limiting your interactions to only what is absolutely necessary. If you must communicate with the narcissist post-separation, you must stand strong on your boundaries, which can be difficult, but it will allow you to remain outside the cycle of abuse, where you continue to remain in control, autonomous, and empowered.

Text and Email Communication Post-Separation

All communication with the narcissist should be in writing whenever possible. This offers you increased control over the dialogue and reduces manipulative strategies such as gaslighting (e.g., "I never said that"). Communication should always involve the following strategies:

- Respond only *to* and *with* facts, while refraining from the use of emotions or opinions.
- Reponses should be short and concise (e.g., yes/no responses, dates, times, places).
- Respond only when necessary (e.g., custody schedule times). If you receive a lengthy text, respond only to the necessary facts or required items, while ignoring accusatory statements, gaslighting tactics, attempts at distraction, and emotional manipulation.
- Keep digital records of electronic communication, such as screenshots of text messages.
- In child custody cases, it can be helpful for you to use parent communication platform apps, such as OurFamilyWizard, to reduce the potential for manipulation and abuse by the narcissistic parent.

REFLECTION

Which of these communication strategies do you already engage in? How have they been helpful?

Of the strategies listed, which ones do you anticipate being most difficult for you? What do you perceive to be barriers?

Are there other tactics you would add to this list?

Limit Communication with Involved "Others"

Post-separation, narcissists will often recruit family members, friends, and others to obtain information from and about you, create chaos, and push your boundaries. It is important to refrain from engaging in dialogue with these external parties. This reduces the likelihood of manipulation, gaslighting, self-doubt, and guilt trips. Examples of how to limit communication include the following:

- Block on social media those in the narcissist's orbit that create and promote chaos.

- When managing in-person interactions with people who enable the narcissist's abusive behaviors, it is helpful to have preestablished responses. Relying on these templates can help you stay composed both outwardly and inwardly during these uncomfortable exchanges, preventing heightened emotions from disrupting your ability to uphold your boundaries in the moment and ultimately depriving the narcissist of the reaction they crave via their flying monkeys. For instance, you might say:
  - "I've made my decision about this."
  - "We will just have to disagree on this."
  - "I am not comfortable with this conversation."
  - "I have to do what's best for me."
  - "I appreciate your concern, but this is between me and [*the narcissist*]."

REFLECTION

List three additional examples of preestablished responses you can use in interactions with those who enable the narcissist's narrative:

1. ______________________________

   ____

2. ______________________________

   ____

3. ______________________________

   ____

Conclusion

Walking away from a narcissistic abusive relationship is rarely straightforward. It is often messy, frightening, and even dangerous. It typically requires multiple attempts before a true separation is possible. Even then, the manipulation and abusive behaviors frequently continue long after the relationship itself has ended. For the narcissist, the people in their world are not seen as autonomous beings, but as objects, each serving a specific purpose and need in their narrative. When this is challenged through separation, it represents a profound loss of control and power for the narcissist, often intensifying their effort to reassert dominance through continued coercion and abuse. The strategies outlined in this chapter are essential tools for navigating your separation from a narcissist with clarity, empowerment, and a strong sense of safety.

8

Starting a New Chapter

One of the most misleading expectations a person can have after escaping a narcissistic abusive relationship is that they should be able to "get over" the trauma they have endured. This assumption can keep people stuck in a vicious cycle of rumination, isolation, shame, and guilt. Over time, this cognitive loop can lead to significant mental health difficulties, such as major depression, anxiety, C-PTSD, substance abuse, and even physical health issues.

Trauma changes you. It shakes the core beliefs you hold about yourself and the world around you. Narcissistic abuse actually rewires your brain's neural pathways, wreaking havoc on your nervous system. To have the expectation that you need to *get over* something so disruptive to your entire being is simply unrealistic.

Now, does this mean that you will never be able to regain your self-identity and move forward into a fulfilled life? Absolutely not. But what it does mean is that these experiences have changed you as a person. To ignore or avoid this reality will do more psychological, cognitive, and physical harm than good. The ongoing trauma you experienced *must* be acknowledged, processed, and ultimately accepted.

Keep in mind that acceptance does *not* mean approving of the abuse or minimizing the harm you experienced. In fact, it is quite the opposite. From an ACT perspective, acceptance in this context involves acknowledging whatever painful thoughts, memories, emotions, or physical sensations arise—without trying to get rid of them or judging yourself for having them. While your willingness to tolerate this discomfort in the moment will not make the pain of your trauma disappear overnight, it will lessen its intensity and frequency over time. By instead choosing to be present with your internal experiences, you reduce the power and influence your trauma has over you.

The Concept of Letting Go

It is a common misconception that "letting go" is synonymous with "getting rid of." We associate healing with the absence of pain—assuming that recovery from a narcissistic relationship requires you to get rid of all negative thoughts and feelings associated with long-term coercive control and abuse. However, as we've seen, this healing journey is a lengthy, sometimes lifelong process of emotional and psychological rebuilding and growth. For example, even if you've done the difficult work to go no contact with a narcissistic parent, you may to some extent always grapple with the impact of their abuse. You may have ended a narcissistic friendship years ago but still find yourself easily triggered or distrustful because of the deep hurt this individual has caused you.

Some behaviors *seem* to have the ability to help you "get rid of" your pain: drinking, using drugs, overeating, chronic worrying, burying yourself in work, and socially isolating are all common maladaptive behaviors people use to avoid feeling their pain. But the benefit will always be short-lived. Gaining temporary relief through avoiding, suppressing, or refusing to acknowledge your pain only keeps you stuck in your struggle. It is as if you are playing tug-of-war and one end of the rope is nailed into the wall—you can pull with all your might, but you will never win, and you'll only become more frustrated and exhausted. But if you were to stop the struggle by dropping the rope, you free yourself up physically, cognitively, and emotionally to attend to the things you value most in life. Is the rope still there? Absolutely. In fact, you are free to pick it up again and struggle with it anytime you want.

If you want to let go, you must be willing to *be present with* what you want to let go. From an ACT standpoint, you must observe the pain as it comes up, sit with it rather than fight against it, and allow it to pass. By focusing all your energy on the struggle, you continue to remain trapped in the very pain you're trying to escape.

Imagine you're loading groceries into your car and notice a piece of gum stuck to your back tire. In trying to remove it, you find it has melted and is now stuck to your nails and fingers. You grab a napkin to wipe it off, but pieces of napkin stick to your hands. Rushing home because of the groceries, you tell yourself you'll deal with it later, but as you pull out of the parking space, sticky bits of napkin and strands of melted gum are now all over your hands and the steering wheel. Once home, you spend the next 30 minutes cleaning melted gum off your steering wheel, your hands, and somehow even your hair. The result? Despite your best effort to clean up the gum, you not only managed to create an even bigger mess, but you've also wasted an hour that could have been spent on something you value, like baking your daughter's birthday cake. But what would have happened if you had simply noticed the gum on your tire and left it alone? You would have avoided the mess and started baking the cake on time—and chances are, you would have forgotten about the gum on your tire. Would the gum still have been stuck to your tire? Yes. But the situation would have been much less frustrating and certainly less messy.

This idea ties directly into mindfulness and ACT-based concepts, which encourage noticing thoughts and emotions without reacting in ways that are inconsistent with your values. By simply allowing them to come up, observing them without judgment, and allowing them to pass, we keep our physical, emotional, and cognitive energy free to focus on the things we value most.

REFLECTION

Describe a time when you avoided or suppressed your emotional pain.

What behaviors did you engage in? Did they help or hurt you? Explain.

Now that you are aware of how avoiding your discomfort only makes it worse, would you handle this situation differently? Explain.

Reassessing Your Values

After leaving a narcissistic relationship, many people have lost their sense of self. Over years of abuse and coercive control, they have lost trust in others and, more importantly, in themselves. They doubt their ability to accurately perceive their reality and have lost sight of their personal preferences, their strengths, and their identity.

This is why a reassessment of personal values is an important first step in the healing process. This functions as the foundation upon which you can base the direction of your healing path. When your world feels like it has been pulled out from under you, relying on your values can help stabilize you amid the chaos. Values serve as the building blocks needed to restore self-identity. Returning again to the ACT concept of values, ask yourself this simple question: "Is this behavior in line with what I value?" Though the answer is a simple yes or no, you can use this question to provide yourself with the scaffolding to stay on a healthy and productive healing path now and into the future.

Behaviors consistent with our values lead to increased feelings of fulfillment in life. Conversely, behaviors that take us in the opposite direction of our values are more likely to result in increased daily stress, dissatisfaction, anxiety, and relationship difficulties.

For example, someone who values being a contributing member of their community might consider their weekly volunteer work at the local library as a behavior that aligns with their value. If this person spent the next four Sundays laying in bed mindlessly scrolling on their phone, their behavior would be taking them further away from their value of contributing to their community. Moving away from their value by repeatedly canceling their volunteer work is more likely to lead to feelings of overall dissatisfaction and guilt, and have a negative impact on both their body and mind.

Rebuilding Your Social Network

Coming out of a narcissistic relationship is not just scary; it is also lonely. As you navigate the process of ending the relationship and moving forward, it is extremely important that you seek some form of social support. This could be family members, friends, coworkers, a support group, or a therapist.

As you adjust to life outside the narcissistic relationship, you will inevitably have moments of doubt, and you may even regret leaving. This is okay! The combination of shame, doubt, gaslighting, hoovering behaviors, and the intermittent nature of the coercive control and abuse itself often leads people to question their perceived reality of the situation: *Was it really* that *bad? What if it was all my fault? What if they really mean that they will change this time?* This thought process, although extremely common, is the exact reason why social support during this time is so critical. A trustworthy and objective third party can help protect you from the influence of gaslighting and other manipulative tactics the narcissist will use to draw you back into their web. Outside support people can provide clarity, offer concrete reminders of why you left, challenge any skewed perceptions you may have of the relationship, and help ground you in the present moment.

REFLECTION

Who would you include in your social network? Why?

____

____

____

What do you foresee as being the biggest obstacle to reconnecting to social support?

____

____

____

Since leaving the relationship, have you noticed any changes in the types of people you turn to for support?

____

____

____

In what ways does your current support differ from those you might have relied on prior to the relationship?

____

____

____

Rebuilding Relationships

With your perception of trust, intimacy, and love distorted by the narcissist's manipulation and coercive control, it's only natural to doubt your own judgment and ability to read others' intentions. This makes it both overwhelming and scary to reconnect with people, regardless of the type of narcissistic relationship you experienced. Having experienced your sense of self-identity stripped away throughout the relationship may have left you believing you have very little to offer in relationships, or that you're unworthy or incapable of healthy connection.

To begin the reconnection process with others, it is necessary to reassess your own relationship values. What do *you* value in your relationships? How do you perceive your worth as a partner, friend, or relative? Reconnecting with others in ways that coincide with your personal relationship values will serve as anchor points along your journey.

REFLECTION

What three things do you value most in a healthy relationship?

1. ______________________________

____

2. ______________________________

____

3. ______________________________

____

What three things do you value most about yourself in relationships?

1. ______________________________

____

2. ______________________________

____

3. ______________________________

____

Dating After Narcissistic Abuse

While each person's healing timeframe is unique, I typically recommend people wait at least a year before they go back into the dating scene. Although healing from narcissistic abuse is a perpetual journey, you need to give yourself the time and space to regain your autonomy and realign with your values and core self before entering another relationship. Rediscovering who you once were, and who you want to be, will help you form healthy, meaningful connections as you navigate the healing process.

Rebuilding confidence in the accuracy and validity of your own feelings and perceptions is a gradual process. It is also completely normal to feel fear and hesitation about placing your trust in a new relationship. Sharing aspects of your dating experiences with trusted friends, family, and your therapist can help you develop a more accurate perception of others' dating behaviors and intentions. This provides you with the emotional and cognitive space to look at a new relationship from a perspective of clarity and accuracy rather than through a distorted lens that has been shaped by the narrative of the narcissist. You should also have open communication with your new partner, sharing your feelings and educating your partner about triggers as they arise. Remember, it is perfectly healthy to be overly cautious in a new relationship. Be patient with yourself and take your time moving forward.

When first reentering the dating world, it is normal to become hyperfocused on potential red flags and misperceive genuine and benign behaviors as evidence of love bombing and coercive control. In fact, your brain is doing exactly what it is intended to do—it's keeping you safe. These triggers vary widely based on personal experiences with narcissistic abuse, ranging from a tone of voice or smell to the pace at which physical intimacy progresses. It is not uncommon for clients to tell me how they flinch at the sight and sound of incoming calls and texts, overanalyze messages from someone they're interested in, and feel bored or unsafe with a sense of calm or peace in a new relationship.

It is essential to identify your triggers without self-judgment, not just for the health of your new relationship but also for your overall healing journey. Keep in mind, a response to a trigger doesn't always show up as a thought or an emotion. Oftentimes, especially with narcissistic abuse survivors, a trigger response can be physiological in nature. This can include a rapid heart rate, shallow breathing, sweating, or even physical pain. For instance, many of my clients describe the sound of footsteps on the staircase as a powerful trigger, bringing on a racing heart and shortness of breath, as it reminds them of their narcissistic abuser approaching the upstairs bedroom, where much of the emotional and psychological abuse occurred. Although these sensations may feel scary, uncontrollable, and confusing, they are not harmful. Your body has been operating in survival mode, and it will take time for your nervous system to regulate and your brain to adjust to new, safer relationship experiences.

Remember, it is important to experience these uncomfortable sensations as they arise in the moment, rather than avoiding them through unhealthy behaviors, like shutting out your partner. This approach will help you learn to tolerate your discomfort without fear and judgment, and, over time, retrain your brain to recognize that they are not harmful and therefore do not need to be avoided. Eventually, this will help regulate your nervous system, create a sense of safety, and empower you to foster and maintain healthy relationships.

REFLECTION

Since escaping a narcissistic abusive relationship, what existing situations, words, or behaviors in your current relationships trigger a strong emotional or physical response in you?

Do your triggers tend to show up more in certain types of relationships (e.g., family, romantic, work)?

Do you notice any patterns in what triggers you (e.g., a particular topic of conversation, behavior, situation, smell, or environment)?

When you notice a trigger, what specific thoughts, emotions, and physical sensations come up for you?

How do your mind and body react in the moment? Do you shut down, become hyper-alert, immediately argue, or quickly apologize?

____

____

____

What strategies and skills have you used that helped you in these moments? What have you used that has not worked or has made it worse?

____

____

____

Select one trigger you've noticed in a current relationship. Then choose one strategy you've learned from this workbook to help you navigate the emotional, cognitive, and physical discomfort that arises when you are exposed to this trigger.

Trigger: ______________________________________

Selected strategy: ______________________________

Describe your experience while using the strategy. What thoughts, physical sensations, or feelings came up for you during this practice? Was the strategy helpful? What other areas within your relationship can it be applied to?

____

____

____

____

____

How Will I Know When I've Healed?

I am asked this question by many of my clients, and my answer never changes: Once you recognize the blueprint of a narcissist's behavior, you can never unsee it. When your brain begins to recognize their behavior patterns, a cognitive shift occurs in your mind. The manipulative tactics that once felt confusing, anxiety provoking, and overwhelming become obvious; you move from being caught in the abuse cycle to becoming an active observer of their playbook. This shift allows you to take back control, anticipate their moves, and respond to their underlying motives rather than reacting to their words and actions at face value.

At first, this might seem like an unattainable goal to you. But soon their predictability will be undeniable, so much so that you may find yourself shaking your head or even laughing at just how scripted and unoriginal their behavior is. That is empowerment. When you can see their behaviors as separate from you and their tactics as painfully predictable, you can set more effective boundaries. You stop waiting for them to change, to apologize, or to acknowledge the harm they've caused you. You no longer feel the need to defend, explain, or justify your very appropriate reactions to their abuse.

At this point, closure stops being something you seek from them, and instead becomes something you give to yourself. You'll see that waiting for closure from the narcissist is just another way for them to maintain power over you, and most importantly, control over your healing. The truth is, they deliberately refuse to give genuine closure. And when you release the need for them to do so, they lose power. Their number appearing on your phone, their posting of new relationships on social media, and even the sound of their voice will no longer have the same impact it once had on your nervous system. What once triggered immense fear and anxiety becomes nothing more than annoying background noise. What once consumed you no longer takes up space without your permission. *That* is freedom from the narcissist.

The narcissist's influence over your daily schedule, decisions, and thoughts grows increasingly irrelevant, and as you disentangle yourself from their control, the narrative they once conditioned you to accept unravels. Each intentional experience and values-driven action you take becomes living proof against the distorted story you were taught to believe. Gradually, your sense of self, identity, and agency will be restored. You reclaim authority over who are and who you want to become, deciding which parts of you are authentically *you* and which were constructed by the narcissist to keep you small. Through consistent support, practice, and lived experiences that contradict the old narrative, your clarity, resilience, and self-identity will undoubtedly return in time.

One of the most powerful steps in healing from narcissistic abuse is giving yourself the space to speak your truth. But because narcissistic abuse and coercive control can feel almost impossible to explain at times, especially to those unfamiliar with its nuances, it can leave you feeling frustrated, misunderstood, and alone. This is exactly why it is critical to reach out to someone you feel safe with and find a therapist who validates and understands the complex layers of this form of abuse—someone who can break apart the nuances of the narcissist's manipulation and controlling intentions. Working with a therapist who specializes in this form of abuse can help you carry your story differently and teach you how to integrate that piece of your history into your life on your own terms. They can guide you in separating who you are from what you experienced and help you shift from shame, guilt, and fear into understanding that your personal narrative exists separately from the narcissist's version of you. It may never feel comfortable to say you were in an abusive relationship. But over time, it will become easier to move forward as you immerse yourself in healthier surroundings and relationships. Moving forward comes from the recognition that speaking your truth and owning it fully is an act of strength, bravery, and healing.

The abuse you endured is not your fault, but healing from it is your responsibility. Setting boundaries, shifting responses, changing behaviors, and taking action to leave an abusive relationship will all feel extremely uncomfortable at first. Not because you are doing something wrong, but because it is unfamiliar and scary. Start small, start slow, and stay consistent—but most importantly, stay safe. Starting small helps you gain a sense of mastery, while remaining consistent creates comfort and familiarity with your new behaviors. Remember, your behavior changes are for *you*. They enable you to walk away from the narcissistic relationship feeling empowered and in control of your emotions, behaviors, thoughts, and life.

Above all, remember that healing from this form of abuse is not something that occurs overnight. It is an ongoing journey of rediscovering your sense of self and reclaiming all that was stolen from you. You are worthy of living a fulfilled life, not just surviving. You did nothing wrong, nor did you deserve to be treated in this way. Taking back your identity, power, and ownership of your life is an essential step in the healing process—and it is exactly that: *a process.*

Final Words

While the journey ahead may not be easy, you now have the understanding and skill set necessary to move forward in your life. Rest assured, there *is* light at the end of the tunnel. While you may not return to the exact person you once were, it is important to know that this is to be expected, and the new "you" is one that is infinitely stronger, more resilient, and equipped with invaluable knowledge about who you are, where you're headed, and what you're willing to tolerate along your journey.

If while reading this book, you've come to recognize yourself, or someone you love, in these abusive dynamics, know that it is never too late to reclaim your power and sense of self. Move along your own path, at your own pace, remembering to pause and give yourself grace along the way. Establish the boundaries and contact levels that feel safest and healthiest for you in this moment, with the understanding that you have the power to shift these limits as you see fit.

It is my hope that this workbook has provided you with a clear framework to better understand the complexities of narcissistic abuse and coercive control while also equipping you with practical tools and strategies to navigate these harmful relationships. Recognizing the patterns of abuse, setting boundaries based on function, and acquiring the skills to navigate the often painful and traumatic end of the relationship are critical steps to healing. The path may not seem obvious at first, and healing may seem like an insurmountable task, but you will be okay. You are resilient. You are a survivor.

Resources

Hotlines

211 (access to local resources and services): call or text 211, or visit 211.org

National Domestic Violence Hotline: call 1-800-799-SAFE, text "START" to 88788, or visit thehotline.org

Books/Articles

"50 Obstacles to Leaving" by Sarah Buel: https://www.thehotline.org/resources/get-help-50-obstacles-to-leaving

A Liberated Mind: How to Pivot Toward What Matters by Steven C. Hayes, PhD

ACT Made Simple: An Easy-to-Read Primer on Acceptance and Commitment Therapy by Dr. Russ Harris

Diagnostic and Statistical Manual of Mental Disorders, Fifth Edition by the American Psychiatric Association

Disarming the Narcissist: Surviving and Thriving with the Self-Absorbed by Wendy T. Behary, LCSW

Find Good Habits: A Workbook for Daily Growth by Jaime Zuckerman, PsyD

Find Your Calm: A Workbook to Manage Anxiety by Jaime Zuckerman, PsyD

Framed: Women in the Family Court Underworld by Dr. Christine M. Cocchiola and Amy Polacko

Get Out of Your Mind and Into Your Life: The New Acceptance and Commitment Therapy by Steven C. Hayes, PhD

It's Not You: Identifying and Healing from Narcissistic People by Ramani Durvasula, PhD

Narcissistic Abuse: A Therapist's Guide to Identifying, Escaping, and Healing from Toxic and Manipulative People by Vanessa M. Reiser, LCSW

Run Like Hell: A Therapist's Guide to Recognizing, Escaping, and Healing from Trauma Bonds by Nadine Macaluso, PhD

When Life Happens: The Mindset Shift You Need to Manage Stress, Build Confidence, and Break Free by Rachel L. Goldman, PhD

Podcasts

Crime Analyst with Laura Richards: https://www.thelaurarichards.com/podcasts

Next Up: Narcissism with Dr. Z: https://www.drjaimezuckerman.com/podcast

Perfect Prey: A Coercive Control Podcast with Dr. Christine M. Cocchiola: https://podcasts.apple.com/us/podcast/perfect-prey-a-coercive-control-podcast/id1704962170

Apps/Websites

Dr. Ramani Network: https://apps.apple.com/us/app/the-dr-ramani-network/id6757620726

National Alliance on Mental Illness: www.nami.org

National Institute of Mental Health: www.nimh.nih.gov

Acknowledgments

This book exists because of the survivors: for those who so often feel unseen, unheard, and misunderstood. Your experiences matter. And your unbelievable strength and resilience, even in moments when you may not feel it, is extraordinary. This book would not be possible without your courage to speak and your willingness to be vulnerable. I am deeply humbled and honored to have been trusted with your stories and a part of your healing journey.

To my clients, thank you. Your bravery and perseverance are the foundation of this book. As a psychologist, your trust is something I hold with the utmost respect and responsibility. One of the greatest privileges of this work, and what I find most fulfilling, is witnessing the moment in therapy when everything finally clicks. It's that unmistakable shift in our work together when the puzzle pieces finally fit and confusion gives way to clarity. All the chaos suddenly makes sense, and you understand the narcissist's blueprint. I can see it in your faces and hear it in your voices. And in that moment, I know you are going to be okay. Something fundamental changes in a way that cannot be unseen or undone. You get *it*. Thank you for allowing me to witness that transformation, again and again. It is, without question, the most rewarding part of the work I do.

I am profoundly grateful to the entire PESI team for giving me the opportunity and platform to bring this important work to life. From the very first conversation with Kate Sample, I still remember our initial call and the shared excitement as this idea began to take shape. To see it come to fruition has been an incredible journey. Thank you for believing in this message and for your unwavering support and patience throughout the process.

To my incredibly brilliant editors, Chelsea Thompson—who I could Zoom with for hours about life—and Alissa Schneider, thank you for your dedication to this project, your patience, and for helping me shape this book into what it has become.

And to my incredible community of colleagues and peers, thank you for your unwavering support and sharing your knowledge. Without your input and feedback, none of this would be possible. I am continually inspired in your presence. A special thank-you to the following colleagues, who have been a source of support, encouragement, friendship, and of course, humor: Dr. Lina Haji, Tina Swithin, Dr. Rachel Goldman, Vanessa Reiser, LCSW, Laura Richards, Mark Vicente, Dr. Christine Cocchiola, Dr. Kerry McAvoy, Dr. Sue Varma, Wendy Behary, LCSW, and Dr. Nadine Macaluso. Thank you for your meaningful contributions to this field and your commitment to advancing the understanding of narcissistic abuse.

I would also like to acknowledge the work of Dr. Steven Hayes, which has had a profound influence on my career. Many years ago, in my doctoral program, I was introduced to acceptance and commitment therapy, a therapeutic framework developed by Dr. Hayes. Over the last two decades, this approach has profoundly shaped my clinical practice as well as my own life. Its emphasis on psychological flexibility and values-based living has been transformative, not only in theory, but in the lives of the people I have had the privilege to work with. This book is a reflection of my mission to apply ACT to the healing journey of survivors of narcissistic abuse to help them move out of the mental entanglement and back into a life guided by meaning and purpose.

Lastly, to my family. Thank you for your endless love, patience, and belief in me. You supported me though long hours, late nights, and the occasional rants. Specifically to my husband, thank you for picking up the pieces while I locked myself away with my laptop for hours. And to my kiddos—G, W, and B—thank you for being patient with me. I know it has been frustrating. But I can tell you this—this book would never have been finished if it wasn't for the hugs, kisses, and occasional impromptu fashion shows in my office.

This book is not mine alone. It is the collective effort of some of the strongest people I know, and I am deeply grateful to each and every one of you who made it possible.

About the Author

Dr. Jaime Zuckerman (Dr. Z) is a licensed clinical psychologist, author, and nationally recognized expert in narcissistic abuse. She is a highly sought-after relationship coach for those experiencing narcissistic abuse in relationships of all types and is the owner of The Z Group, a private group therapy practice located outside of Philadelphia, PA, specializing in anxiety, depression, and complex relationship dynamics.

Dr. Z is an influential social media personality in the mental health space and a frequent media contributor. She has been featured in numerous print and digital platforms, including *Huffington Post*, *The Washington Post*, *The New York Times*, and Oprah Daily. She also appears regularly on both local and national TV news programs, such as Court TV, Fox Philly, CBS Philly, and Good Day Philadelphia. She is a frequent guest on well-known podcasts, including *When Reality Hits with Brittany Cartwright*, *The Skinny Confidential*, the Foster sisters' *The World's First Podcast*, and *The Sabrina Zohar Show*. Dr. Z is the author of two bestselling interactive workbooks: *Find Your Calm*, focused on managing anxiety, and *Find Good Habits*, geared toward daily goal setting and personal growth.

Links

Website: https://www.drjaimezuckerman.com

The Z Group: https://www.zgrouptherapy.com

Next Up: Narcissism podcast: https://www.drjaimezuckerman.com/podcast

Books

https://www.drjaimezuckerman.com/books

Social Media

Instagram: https://www.instagram.com/dr.z_psychologist

YouTube: https://www.youtube.com/@DrJaimeZuckerman

TikTok: https://www.tiktok.com/@dr.z_psychologist